U0903094

陕西历史博物馆珍藏

Selected Treasures of Shaanxi History Museum

金银器

主编 申秦雁 /Editor-in-Chief Shen Qinyan

陕西人民美术出版社 西安 /SHAANXI PEOPLE'S FINE ARTS PUBLISHING HOUSE XI'AN

目录

Contents

前言
Preface

陕西历史博物馆是中国第一座现代化的国家级博物馆，占地6.5万平方米，建筑面积5.56万平方米，馆藏文物37万件，一级文物达762件（组）。作为综合性博物馆，所藏文物门类众多，以青铜器、金银器、唐墓壁画、陶俑最具特色。其中金银器有1000余件，时代跨度从西周早期到清代晚期。尤以陕西神木出土的匈奴金银器和西安何家村、西安电车二场工地、耀县柳林出土的唐代金银器最具代表性，它们不仅享誉国内，在世界艺术之林中，也占有重要地位。

陕西历史博物馆内装备有先进的中央空调、大型变配电、计算机管理、安全检测、防火防盗系统和六种语言的同声传译系统。十年来，已接待国内外观众500多万人次。文物展出足迹遍及日本、韩国、新加坡、美国、墨西哥、英国、法国、芬兰、摩纳哥等国。

Shaanxi History Museum, with a coverage area of 65,000 sq metres, and a construction area of 55,600 sq metres, is the first modernized museum with perfect equipments, including sophisticated central air-conditioning system, large power supply systen, security check, fire proof system, and a simultaneous translation system of six languages. It boasts for a rich collection of 370,000 pieces of cultural relics, 762 belong to the first-class relics. As a comprehensive museum, the collection is great of variety, such as bronzes, gold and silvers and the mural paintings from the Tang dynasty tombs, and pottery figures are typical. Among which, there are more than 1000 pieces of gold and silver wares ranging from the early Western Zhou dynasty to the late Qing dynasty. The most important discoveries include the hoard from Hejiacun building site in the southern suburbs of Xi’an city, Shenmu finds of Hun minority (Xiongnu) in the northern Shaanxi province, the finds at Beiyin village, Liulin, Yaoxian county, and the site in No.2 Trolley Lot, Xi’an city. All these excavations not only enjoy a high fame at home, but also occupy a very important position in the forest of arts of the world.

Since the opening to the public in 1991, this museum has received more than 5 million visitors. The tour exhibitions of selected objects have ever been held almost all over the world, such as Nippon, South Korea, Singapore, the Untied States, Mexico, Great Britain, France, Finland and Monaco.

申秦雁

中国古代金银器概述

一

金有黄色的美丽光泽，化学性能很稳定，耐腐蚀，不易被氧化，即使长期存在于空气和水中也没有什么变化。金还有良好的导电性和导热性，延展性也非常好。1克纯金可以拉成直径为0.00434毫米、长3500米的金丝；1克纯金还可以锤辗成厚度仅有0.23×10^{-6}毫米的金箔。金的密度为19.3，是最重的金属之一。金还是非常耐高温的金属，它的熔点达1064.43℃。金在地壳中的含量只有十万万分之五，分布也很分散，一吨金矿石，往往只含有几克、十几克的金，属稀有的贵重金属。金的化学符号Au，据说来自拉丁文Aurora（曙光）一词。

银有白色的光泽，化学性能较稳定，不易被氧化，但对硫有很强的亲和性，容易与硫直接发生作用。银的导电性和导热性在金属中居第一位。银的延展性也比较好，易于拉丝和锤辗成片。银的熔点为960℃，也是耐高温金属。银在地壳中的丰度大约是金的15倍，但通常很少以自然状态存在，因此是仅次于金的贵重金属。银的化学符号Ag，据说来自梵文Arganta（明亮）一词。

金和银是自然界中发现的最古老的金属元素之一。世界各大古老民族在其文明之初，几乎都与金银发生了不解之缘，可以说，金和银在各古老民族的文化发展中都起过相当重要的作用。由于金银的稀有贵重，各个民族都将其视为珍宝，彼此间进行攫取和占有。也正是由于金银的稀有贵重，人们佩戴和使用金银制作的装饰品和器物，就成为身份与等级的标志、权力和财富的象征了。不仅生前使用，甚至死后也将其带入坟墓，“他们深信，自己生时埋了的金银，对他们死后在另一个世界里有用。”[1]

关于金银，在世界文化史中曾经留下许多脍炙人口的故事，其中最著名的要算阿基米德测定金冠的故事了。传说古希腊时，国王锡拉古命令宫廷首饰匠用纯金打制一顶王冠，事后疑心匠人掺假，但又不想毁坏王冠，于是请来科学家阿基米德检验。阿基米德苦思冥想无法得知金冠是否掺假。后来他在澡堂洗澡，从水溢的现象中受到启发，根据重量、体积、比重的关系，测定出王冠的含金量，最后得出工匠以假换真的结论。这一发现，经总结验证成为科学史上著名的阿基米德浮力定律。

关于金银器的解释，一般来讲有广义的和狭义的两种。广义的泛指用金银制成的一切物品，而狭义的仅指用金银制作的器皿。广义的金银器，是学者研究时普遍关注的对象；狭义的金银器，则是学者研究的重点对象。中国古代金银制品的出现，从目前考古发现来看，是在四千多年前，相当于夏的时代，比如甘肃玉门火烧沟墓地出土的金耳环、金银制鼻饮[2]，辽宁敖汉旗夏家店下层文化遗址出土的金耳环[3]。这几件早期的金银制品，虽然铸造粗糙，成分复杂，但它给予我们的启示有两点是很清楚的：一是古人已经掌握了金银的原始冶炼铸造方法，二是金银制品的使用，从一开始就与原始的审美观以及原始的宗教观相结合，这一点对以后金银制品的使用有着至关重要的影响。春秋战国时期，随着生产力的进一步发展，金银的使用也更为广泛，不仅小件饰品普遍增多，而且还出现了器皿，如湖北随县曾侯乙墓就出土有5件金质器皿[4]，其中的金盏，重2.15公斤，制作工艺非常精湛，含金量也高达98%，说明当时的楚国已经掌握了制作大型金质器皿的高超技术，这在中国古代金银器发展史上具有划时代意义。这一时期，错金银工艺、鎏金工艺和镶嵌工艺也开始出现。秦汉时期，金银用量明显增大，在秦始皇陵二号铜车马上，仅发现的金质饰件就有747件，银质的有817件。汉代，皇帝动辄以黄金赏赐大臣，官吏之间祝寿、贿赂也多用黄金，上流社会流行使用金银器或金银釦器，这种时尚与道家方术思想的影响有关："祠灶则致物，致物而丹砂可化为黄金，黄金成以为饮食器则益寿，益寿而海中蓬莱仙者可见，见之以封禅则不死，黄帝是也。"[5] 金银器的使用被蒙上了浓厚的政治、宗教色彩。魏晋南北朝时期，金银器种类明显增多，装饰制作也趋于精细，中西文化交流和南北文化融合在金银器中有明显的反映，佛教内容也出现在金银器的装饰上。隋唐时期，是中国古代金银器发展的高峰时期，由于道教盛行，人们笃信金银能辟邪、防毒，使人延年益寿、长生不老，因此皇室贵族极其讲究使用金银器。在对西方金银器经过拿来、模仿、消化、吸收之后，形成了自己绚丽多姿、成熟健康、优雅活泼的风格，成为一代盛世的重要标志。宋代，随着城市经济的繁荣，民间私营的金银器制作行业兴盛起来，金银器上多砸印有金银店铺和工匠名号以及金子或银子的成色。银器的使用已经民间化，装饰上由于融入了绘画艺术而充满了诗情画意。辽代金银器有浓郁的民族特色，如以金银为面具，铜丝络手足的奇异葬俗，适合于游牧民族狩猎生活的鸡冠壶、提梁壶等器型。元代，民间银器制作非常发达，出现了一批著名的银工和精美的作品，如朱碧山和他的银槎杯。明清时期，金银器的造型和制作讲究美观和精细，以至流于繁琐。金银器上多镶嵌珍珠、宝石，金银工艺还与漆器、木器、玉器等工艺相结合，创造出一系列艺术效果颇为奇胜的合璧产品，开辟了金银器发展的新领域。

中国古代金银器从其来源来看，大致有两种：传世的和出土的。传世的主要是清朝皇宫遗留下来的宫廷用物，数量不多。大量的古代金银器来自考古发现，而考古发现绝大多数又出自窖藏和地宫，遗址和墓葬出土的大多比较零散。解放前，中国境内出土的金银器，多数都经非法渠道流入到欧美、日本等地。据一些学者统计，仅唐代金银器，流散到国外的就有数十件[6]。解放后，伴随着中国考古学的飞速发展，古代金银器也有了惊人的发现，如 1958年北京明定陵出土金器289件、银器271件[7]，1964年陕西西安沙坡唐代窖藏出土银器15件[8]，1970年陕西西安何家村唐代窖藏出土金银器271件[9]，1982年江苏丹徒丁卯桥唐代窖藏出土银器千余件[10]，1985年广东遂溪南朝窖藏出土金银器107件[11]，内蒙古哲里木辽陈国公主墓出土金银器178件[12]，1987年陕西扶风法门寺唐代地宫出土金银器121件[13]，1997年新疆伊犁昭苏古墓出土西突厥金银器40多件[14]。据粗略统计，从1950年到2000年，在全国28个省、市、自治区的170多个市（县）出土的古代金银器，数量约万余件，其时代由夏代一直延续到清代，种类繁多，内涵丰富，涉及到古代政治、经济、军事、宗教、艺术、科技等各个方面，而且由于是科学发掘，一般都是地层清楚，年代明确，科学性强，具有很高的学术价值，已经成为研究中国古代社会尤其是科技史的重要实物资料。陕西是中国古代历史演变的重要舞台，作为13个王朝建都之地的西安，也以出土大量珍贵文物而享誉海内外。目前，从唐代窖藏、地宫、墓葬中出土的金银器大约有40批，其中一半就集中在西安及其附近地区，最重要的是沙坡村窖藏、何家村窖藏和法门寺地宫这三批。它们分别代表了初唐、盛唐、晚唐三个时期，已经成为研究唐代历史的重要依据。

二

中国古代金银器，类型多种多样，涉及范围非常广泛，从其用途来看，可以分为生活器皿、服饰、宗教用具、殡葬用具、动物形装饰品、医药保健用具、车马具、钱币、工具九大类，以前六类为多见。另外还有祭祀、兵器、模型等类，但都极少见。

1.生活器皿

生活器皿是金银器中所占比例最大的一类，也是与人类生存关系最为直接、最为密切的一类。主要有饮食用的杯、盏、盅、盘、碗、碟、壶、锅、鼎、羽觞、箸、匙，盥洗用的洗、匜 、盆，盛放物品的罐、瓶、盒，家居陈设用的花瓶、装饰盘、灯、熏炉、熏球、唾盂、渣斗、镜架等。以杯、碗、盘、壶、盒、盆为多见。

杯：金银杯是古代使用最早的金银器皿之一。早在公元前4世纪，希腊军队的指挥官就讲究使用银杯喝水，也几乎是同一时期，在中国发达富裕的楚国地域出现了国君使用的金杯。使用金银杯除了其质地的高贵外，恐怕也与其消毒、防腐的特殊功能有关。南北朝时期，金银杯的造型多样化起来，而且充满异域风采，如山西大同北魏封和突墓出土的银耳杯、银高足杯[15]，河北赞皇东魏李希宗墓出土的银杯[16]。唐代，金银杯的造型更为丰富，既有以往常见的圆形、椭圆形，也新出现了花瓣形、多棱形，装饰上既充满了异国情调，又洋溢出本土风情(图版28、29)。宋代，仍然流行几何式的多边形和仿生式的花瓣形。江苏溧阳宋代窖藏出土的一件双兽耳银杯，是这一时期新出现的仿古造型[17]。宋代金银杯的制作多用夹层合成法，装饰上也充满诗情画意。元明时期，金银杯在造型上的仿生性更明显也更成熟，如安徽合肥元代窖藏出土的金杯，做成带柄的半柿形[18]。著名银工朱碧山就极擅长制作蟹杯、虾杯，从流行至今的银槎杯就不难看出其水平。湖南通道南明窖藏出土的7件银杯，全部做成立体的枝叶盘绕的蟠桃形[19]。珍藏在北京故宫博物院的“金瓯永固”金杯[20]，是清朝皇帝在每年正月初一的开笔仪式上使用的酒杯，宫廷重要的礼器，从造型和用途上看都有浓重的复古味道。

碗：早期金银制作的碗几乎不见，南北朝时期，中国境内出现了异域风格的银碗，如广东遂溪南朝窖藏出土的莲花纹银碗[21]，山西大同北魏遗址出土的刻花银碗[22]。唐代金银碗发现极多，仅何家村窖藏出土的就达60件。唐代金银碗的造型有圆形、海棠形、多曲花瓣形，有的还仿照民间蒲篮设计。唐以后，比较有特色的金银碗是浙江永嘉出土的宋代兽面纹碗[23]，内蒙古昭乌达盟巴林右旗出土的辽代八棱錾花银温碗[24]，内蒙古临河高油房古城出土的西夏凤凰纹金碗[25]，北京定陵出土的明代牡丹纹银碗[26]。北京故宫博物院珍藏的银胎绿珐琅靶碗[27]，是六世班禅罗布藏巴勒垫伊西到北京时进献给清代皇帝的，代表了清时西藏金银器的风格。

盘：山东临淄武乡窝托村西汉陪葬坑中出土的刻有铭文“秦始皇三十三年”的鎏金盘龙纹银盘[28]，是目前所见时代最早的金银盘，也是迄今为止唯一刻有秦代纪年的银盘，制作工艺也相当成熟。此后零星出土的几件银盘，明显地是舶来物，如山西大同封和突墓出土的鎏金狩猎纹银盘[29]和甘肃靖远北滩乡出土的鎏金人物纹银盘[30]。唐代，金银盘的制作有了空前的发展，从形制上看，有圆形、菱形、花瓣式多曲（四曲、五曲、六曲）形、桃形、荷叶形，盘底也有平底、圜底、矮圈足、高圈足、三足、四足等多种。有的还在口沿部垂饰一周流苏，显得富丽、典雅。唐代还出现直径85.3厘米的特大型银盘（图版46）。值得一提的是，唐代的一些银盘，可能不是实用器而是摆设用装饰盘，如图版40。宋元明时期，流行“画盘”，一件银盘往往就是一幅完整的山水画或人物画，有的还集诗书画于一体，艺术格调非常高雅，这应该是兴盛的文人画给予金银器制作上的一种深刻影响。这种“画盘”的源头，可以追溯到唐代。

壶：目前发现时代较早的是宁夏固原北周李贤墓出土的鎏金银壶（瓶）[31]，一些专家经过考证，认为它是4～5世纪巴克特利亚制品，属萨珊系金银器[32]。唐代出现的鎏金舞马衔环纹银壶（图版79）、鸳鸯蔓草纹金壶[33]，都是极具特色的精品。辽代金银壶较多见，既有波斯萨珊风格的银执壶[34]，又有北方游牧民族风格的鸡冠壶、鱼龙提梁壶[35]。北京明代李伟夫妇墓出土的六角錾花错金执壶[36]，北京故宫博物院珍藏的云龙纹葫芦式金执壶[37]，则反映了明清时期金银壶的造型和装饰特点。

盒：目前所见时代最早的金银盒，是出土于河北满城西汉刘胜墓的银盒[38]，以后历代均有发现，但以唐代金银盒最多见，造型和装饰也最丰富，仅何家村窖藏一次就出土金银盒29件，许多金银盒上保留有珍贵的墨书题记。唐代金银盒从造型上看，有圆、椭圆、方、菱弧、多曲花瓣、云头、半月、瓜棱、蚌壳、卧兽等形状，装饰题材也涉及动物、植物、几何图案、自然风景等各个方面。江苏丹徒丁卯桥窖藏出土的鎏金双凤纹银盒[39]，腹径31厘米，是目前所见唐代最大的银盒。浙江衢州南宋墓出土的银丝盒[40]，设计奇特，制作精巧，是唐之后少见的精品。尤其是内置金质裸体娃娃，展现了宋代供奉吉祥物摩睺罗的社会风俗。

盆：目前所见最早的金银盆出现于唐代，陕西西安何家村窖藏出土的两件金盆（图版7），印证了唐代文献中有关皇室洗儿、嫔妃洗手等使用金盆的记载。与此同时出土的浅腹大银盆（图版4），可能是与匜配套使用的盛水器。陕西扶风法门寺地宫出土的鎏金双鸳团花纹银盆，口径达46厘米，是迄今所见最大的唐代银盆。唐之后，金银盆极少发现，江苏溧阳宋代窖藏出土的鎏金凹花双鱼纹银盆[41]，北京明定陵出土的二龙戏珠纹金盆[42]和北京故宫博物院珍藏的清代双凤戏莲纹金盆[43]，可以说是少见的代表作。

2.服饰

服饰与人类文明有着密不可分的关系，是一个民族精神风貌和文化内涵的重要体现，金银质地的服饰，按用途大致可分为首饰、带饰和佩饰。

①首饰：包括冠饰、发饰、颈饰、耳饰和手饰。人类劳动智慧注入金银之初，就是首先用于制作首饰以美化人类个体的，这个传统一直延续至今。金银首饰以冠饰和发饰发现最多。

冠饰：山西石楼殷商墓葬中出土的带状圈形金头饰[44]，是目前所知年代最早的金冠饰。内蒙古杭锦旗阿鲁柴登战国时期匈奴墓出土的一套鹰形金冠饰[45]，是匈奴文化中最具代表性的金银珍品，也是迄今发现的唯一的一件“胡冠”。魏晋南北朝时期，北方少数民族流行金饰冠，在辽宁北票晋墓[46]、北燕冯素弗墓[47]、内蒙古达茂旗北魏墓[48]中都出土有花枝状或牛头树枝状的金冠饰。辽宋时期，开始出现完整的金银冠[49]，如辽宁建平和朝阳辽墓中出土的二龙戏珠鎏金银冠和双凤戏珠鎏金银冠，据分析，可能是墓主生前担任萨满巫师所使用的法器——神帽。明代，金银冠饰更为多见，其中品级最高者是北京定陵出土的万历皇帝生前所戴的金翼善冠[50]。

发饰：常见的有簪、钗。北京平谷商代墓葬中出土的金笄，是至今所见最早的金银制发饰。魏晋南北朝时期，开始流行金银簪，唐代簪头出现各种造型，宋代簪头的变化更为多样，簪杆上还多砸印出铺号。明代，金银簪的制作达到登峰造极的地步，簪头的造型和装饰，既有人物楼阁、花草动物，又有极富民间色彩的吉祥物，制作工艺也更为繁复、精细，如北京西郊李伟墓出土的金凤簪、人物花簪、火焰纹花簪[51]，四川平武王玺墓出土的人物楼阁银簪、女神弹琵琶银簪[52]。北京明定陵出土的双鸾金簪、双层蝴蝶金簪、塔形金簪、玉佛金宝簪[53]，则是这一时期的代表作。从吉林通榆清代公主墓出土的金龙簪、金松竹梅簪、宝石金簪[54]以及北京西郊清墓出土的金凤簪[55]来看，清代金银簪与明代有着一脉相承的关系。

金银钗的发展与金银簪的发展有着大致相同的轨迹。

②带饰：主要有带钩和带具。

带钩：良渚文化遗址中就出土有玉带钩。春秋战国至汉代，流行金属制作的带钩，以金银制作的最为精美。如陕西宝鸡春秋晚期秦国墓出土的盘蛇纹金带钩[56]，七条大小不同有动有静的蛇巧妙地组合在小小的钩面上，紧凑而富有变化，不失为早期黄金制品的佳作。河南辉县固围村战国墓出土的包金镶玉嵌琉璃银带钩[57]，造型硕大而秀丽，装饰上采用鎏金、镶嵌、錾刻、漆绘等多种手法，将白银、黄金、琉璃、白玉等不同色彩、不同质地的材料组合在一起，创造出既对比强烈、富有变化，又和谐适中的装饰效果。江苏涟水三里墩西汉墓出土的战国交龙双凤纹金带钩[58]，造型丰满、厚重，熟练地运用錾花、镶嵌工艺，在同一质地上创造出多层次、多色调的装饰效果，为古代金银带钩中的精品。

带具：有带扣、带板、铊尾等，以带板为多见。带板又叫带銙、带胯。带銙是带面上镶嵌的装饰物，有金、银、铜、玉等不同质地，数量也多少不一，质地和数量因身份等级不同而有所差异，装饰图案也随时代发展而有所变化。先秦至汉代，西南及北方的少数民族就有使用动物纹金银带饰的习俗，如云南晋宁石寨山滇墓出土的有翼虎纹银带扣[59]。在吉林和龙渤海墓曾出土一套由金带扣和18件带銙、2件金铊尾组成的金带饰[60]，金銙精雕细刻并镶嵌有水晶、绿松石等。四川什邡曾出土一件晚唐时期的金腰带[61]，带身刻有十二生肖及缠枝花等，由此可以看出唐代金带饰的风格。蹀躞带是契丹族最具特色的传统服饰，在内蒙古、辽宁等地的辽墓中，都出土有金银蹀躞带。其中以辽宁朝阳前窗户村出土的鎏金戏童纹银带[62]和内蒙古哲里木陈国公主墓出土的金銙银蹀躞带[63]最具特色。从辽宁鞍山崔胜墓出土的鎏金錾花银革带[64]和四川平武王玺墓出土的金带板[65]以及北京明定陵出土的镶珠宝金带饰[66]来看，明代金银带具也是十分考究的。

③佩饰：和带饰一样，除了实用功能以外，还起着美化装饰的作用，同时，它也是身份等级的重要标志。早期，金银佩饰发现的很少，唐之后渐渐多起来。金银佩饰中刀、针等工具类的少见，装饰用的盒、香熏较为多见，其中，无论是造型还是工艺，香熏又是最有代表性的。如内蒙古哲里木辽陈国公主墓出土的金荷包[67]，福建福州和江西德安南宋墓出土的鎏金银香熏[68]，江西南城明朱祐槟墓[69]和北京明定陵出土的金香熏[70]，无一不精巧玲珑、美妙绝伦。

3.宗教用具

金银质地的宗教用具，绝大多数是佛教遗物，道教及其他教派的都极少见。从目前发现的金银佛教用具来看，主要有造像、舍利葬具、法器和供养器，从年代来看，大多集中于唐宋时期。

造像：金银器物中最早出现佛像的是辽宁北票北燕冯素弗墓出土的金饰片。魏晋南北朝时期，比较多见的是鎏金铜造像。唐代出现精美的金银造像，如陕西扶风法门寺唐代地宫出土的鎏金珍珠装捧真身菩萨。宋代还出现了小巧精致的微雕造像，如浙江宁波天封塔地宫出土的一件高8厘米的银佛龛内，站立一尊高仅有1.9厘米的金佛像[71]，雕刻精细准确。内蒙古临河出土罕见的西夏金佛像[72]，河北固安金代宝严寺塔基地宫出土的金、银菩萨立像[73]，则是难得一见的金代精品。北京故宫博物院珍藏的清代金四臂观音像[74]，高80厘米，神态优美，制作精细，是少见的大型金造像。

舍利葬具：金银舍利葬具，从形制来看，有罐、瓶、盒、精舍、柜、棺、椁，以棺椁最为多见，主要流行于唐代、宋代。唐代的金银棺椁一般为前高后低的长方形，长度多在5～20厘米之间，装饰内容以莲花、团花、菩萨、弟子、飞天、仙鹤等为主。著名的有陕西临潼庆山寺塔基出土的一套金棺银椁[75]和扶风法门寺地宫出土的鎏金双凤纹银棺[76]。宋代金银棺椁的形制与唐代相似，只是装饰上佛教内容的图案更为世俗化，如河南邓州福胜寺塔地宫出土的金棺银椁[77]。

法器：金银质的法器发现的主要有锡杖、钵盂、阏伽瓶、如意、法轮、净瓶、金刚杵等。以陕西扶风法门寺唐代地宫出土的银金花双轮十二环锡杖、迎真身纯金钵盂[78]等级最高，制作最精。另外，云南下关出土的南诏国丰佑时期的银金刚杵[79]，河北正定天宁寺凌霄塔地宫出土的宋代的鎏金银净瓶[80]，北京故宫博物院珍藏的镶彩石金曼达也是珍贵的金银法器。

供养器：据佛经记载，供养器有十供：香、花、灯、果、涂、茶、食、宝、珠、衣。从目前发现的金银供养器来看，有宝函、菩萨像、香案、灯、茶具、熏炉、花、珠、牌、幡、塔、殿等。其中陕西扶风法门寺唐代地宫出土的5件银宝函和一套完整的金银茶具[81]，北京房山辽塔出土的银佛幡[82]，河北定县静众寺宋代舍利塔基出土的银塔、木雕贴金莲花[83]和浙江宁波天封塔宋代地宫出土的荷叶荷莲浑银牌[84]，河北固安金代宝严寺塔基地宫出土的银八棱熏炉[85]，都是极为珍贵的供养器。

4.殡葬用具

金银玉石由于其特有的自然属性，被古人赋予了种种美好的希望。以此来作殡葬用具，既是保护尸体的一种需要，也是死者在阴间冥府身份等级的一种象征。金银质的殡葬用具，大致可分为葬服和冥器两类。

葬服：在汉代，皇帝和高级贵族的葬服，流行使用金缕玉衣、银缕玉衣，如河北满城西汉中山靖王刘胜墓出土一套完整的金缕玉衣[86]，使用的金丝金条就有1100克。宁夏固原唐代史道德墓出土一副完整的金覆面饰件[87]，有护额饰、护眉饰、护鼻饰、护耳饰、护嘴饰等，是目前所见惟一的一套唐代金覆面。辽代，契丹贵族有“用金银为面具，铜丝络其手足”的葬俗，内蒙古哲里木陈国公主墓出土了一套由鎏金银冠、金面具、银丝网络、金花银枕、金花银靴等组成的殡葬服饰[88]。浙江衢州南宋墓出土的银鞋[89]，江西德安南宋墓出土的银下颌托、银护膝、银护肘[90]，也都是专为死者制作的葬服。内蒙古巴林右旗还出土一套清代蒙古贵族的金银葬具[91]。

冥钱：墓葬中随葬的金银冥器，发现的有银俑、金灶、银灶、银棒等，但都极为少见。隋唐时期的墓葬中，就发现有随葬金银钱币的现象，明清时期，达官贵人的墓葬中，常常可以见到作为厌胜的各种金银冥钱，直径一般在1～5厘米左右，大多制作得单薄、粗糙。钱的正面多有4个字的铭文，内容多为吉祥语，如四川剑阁明代赵炳然墓出土的“贞节贤良”、“长命富贵”金钱[92]，北京明定陵出土的“吉祥如意”、“消灾延寿”金钱[93]。有的吉祥语还有明显的佛教色彩，如江西南城明代朱由木墓出土的“金光接引”、“径上西天”金钱[94]，甘肃兰州上西园明墓出的“法轮转迴”金钱[95]。

5.动物形装饰品

用金银制成动物形的装饰品，在春秋时期就已经出现了，如图版135的金啄木鸟，以后各代都有发现。主要形象有虎、豹、龙、羊、刺猬、鹰、蚕、蟾蜍等，有的是其他器物上的装饰附件，有的则是单独的装饰品。战国至汉代，北方的匈奴族流行使用金银制作的动物形装饰品，出现了一些造型新颖独特的艺术品，如图版143的鹿形金怪兽。在江苏盱眙西汉窖藏中，出土一件重9千克，含金量高达99%的金豹[96]，其造型古朴奇特，制作也相当精湛，是罕见的大型动物形金制品，也是目前国内考古发掘出土的最重的一件金器。在云南大理崇圣寺主塔塔顶发现的鎏金镶珠银金翅鸟[97]，取自印度传说，是专镇海中龙妖水怪的保护神，其形象凶猛，刚健有力，熟练地运用多种工艺精制而成，是古大理国极其珍贵的艺术品。

除了动物形装饰品以外，还有用作房间摆设的诗文牌、图画盘等工艺品，其装饰也不限于动物纹了。

6.医药保健用具

有医针、灌药器、贮药器、煎药器、服药器、蒸馏消毒盘、疝气托等。陕西西安何家村唐代窖藏出土大量金银药具[98]，有贮藏药物的盒、罐，煎药的铛、锅，炼丹用的石榴罐，服药的杯、碗，以及朱砂、钟乳等药物，是中国古代金银医药用具最集中最完整的一次发现。

三

中国古代金银器的制作加工属细工，有一整套复杂的精细的工艺。中国古代金银制作工艺，在秦汉之前，基本上处于青铜铸造工艺的范畴，秦汉之后，在西方金银器的影响下，技艺逐渐丰富完善，其工艺主要有范铸、锻打捶揲、錾花、鎏金、镂空、掐丝编织、炸珠、焊接、铆接、旋切、抛光、锥刺、错金银、金银平脱等数十种。一件精美的金银器，往往需要使用多种工艺才可最后完成。可以说，金银器是科技价值含量最高的文物门类之一。

1.范铸

范铸是金银器成型加工所用的一种工艺，它是仿照青铜器铸造工艺发展起来的，也是战国之前主要的成型方法。其程序是：先将所要制作的器型制模翻范，然后将熔炼成液体状的金或银倒入范中，冷却后即成器物。器型简单者一次即可铸成，如图版139的双驼纹金牌饰。复杂者则先分铸，然后再组合成一体，如图版77的银石榴罐。

2.锻打捶揲

锻打捶揲是金银器成型工艺和装饰工艺常用的方法之一。将熔炼提纯后的金块或银块加热，用锤子反复敲打，使其延伸展开成为一定厚度的金片或银片，然后剪裁成所需要的简单器型，如图108的金耳坠。也有将金片、银片剪裁成各种图案作装饰的，如图39金杯坯腹部的花纹。或者将金片银片放置在事先做好的模具中，反复捶打，成为所需要的各种器型，如图版153的银香囊，中间的金香盂，为直径2.8厘米的半球状，内侧无痕，外侧布满捶击点，显然是将厚1毫米的金片，放置在球状砧子上，然后用小锤反复敲打成型，最后用剪刀剪齐边缘。金银器上凸起的花纹图案，也采用捶揲法加工，唐代晚期开始流行，如图版106的银粉盒，盒盖面上的鹦鹉纹就是放在模具上敲打出来的。宋元时期这种浮雕式的敲花工艺极为流行。

3.錾花

錾花是金银器装饰工艺常用的方法之一。其方法是使用各种大小不同的錾具，用小锤敲打錾具，使其沿着预先设计的纹路行走。由于錾头不同，角度不同，錾痕便成为各种不同的花纹轮廓，然后再在轮廓内錾出细密的圆点或圆圈构成地纹（俗称鱼子纹、珍珠纹）。这样形成点线面的结合，加之鎏金工艺的使用，就有了很强的装饰效果，是唐代金银器非常流行的一种装饰方法。

4.刻划

刻划是金银器装饰工艺方法之一。在已经制作成型的器物表面，用刻刀按照预先设定的图案，轻轻划出浅浅的、粗细不一的各种线条花纹，如图版94的银盒，盖面上线刻出展翅欲飞的凤凰，线条细腻流畅，风格简洁明快，造型生动传神，与唐代石椁上的线刻画有类似效果。也有以刻划作为辅助手法来装饰图案细部的，如图版10双鱼纹银碗鱼尾、鳍等细微处都是刻划出来的。

5.鎏金

鎏金亦称涂金、火镀金，是中国古代金属装饰工艺方法之一。先将金和水银合成金汞剂，均匀地涂抹在器物表面，然后通过烘烤加热，让其中的水银蒸发掉，使金附着在器物表面，最后用压子在鎏金面上反复磨压，使之平整、牢固和光亮。战国时就已出现涂金工艺，但多用于银器表面的装饰。汉代出现花镀工艺，在同一器物上，有的部分镀金，有的部分镀银，金银相间，黄白辉映，纹饰华丽，如河北满城汉墓出土的银当卢，陕西兴平茂陵从葬坑出土的鎏金银竹节铜熏炉。唐代银器，主题纹饰多鎏金，称金花银器。

6.镂空

镂空是金银器装饰工艺方法之一。在制作成型的金银器上，用锋利的刻刀按照设计的图案花纹进行镌刻，使之透空，形成有地无地虚实相间的布局，具有神秘、空灵的效果。这种方法多用于熏炉、香囊、钗头的图案装饰，如图版114、152、153。可能是受石刻平级减地手法的影响而出现的。也有通过浇铸而非镌刻形成镂空效果的，如图版140的双鹿纹金牌饰，是将模具做成高低起伏的纹样，金液倒进去后，流入低处，高处即空，形成斑驳陆离的镂空效果，但此法很少见。

7.掐丝、编织

掐丝、编织是金银器成型及装饰工艺方法之一。金和银有很好的延展性，捶打成薄片后，可以剪裁成粗细不等的丝或条，用金丝（条）或银丝（条）编织成一定形状的器物或饰件，形成外观细密、内里透空的效果。汉代这种工艺就已经出现，唐代已经很成熟了。陕西临潼庆山寺地宫出土的唐代金棺银椁，棺盖上有用银丝作成的螺旋塔式装饰，扶风法门寺地宫出土的金银丝结条笼子就是采用这种工艺制成的。另外，将金丝盘编掐制成一定的花纹图案，然后焊接在器物表面形成美丽的装饰，有的还将宝石琉璃等物镶嵌在其中，具有色彩斑斓的视觉效果。这种工艺在汉代就已经出现了，唐代称此为“金筐宝钿”，目前发现最早的唐代金筐宝钿实物是陕西咸阳底张湾武德四年贺若氏墓出土的金耳坠和金梳背，图版27的金筐宝钿团花纹金杯也是采用这种工艺制作的。明清时期流行的各种花丝工艺，如搓花丝、掐花丝、螺丝、祥丝、组丝、编织以及围松等，就是在此基础上发展起来的。

8.炸珠

炸珠是金银器装饰工艺方法之一。先将黄金熔化成液体状，然后通过孔径相同的过滤网，将金液滴入冷水中，使之冷却凝结成直径相同的小金珠。也可以把金碎屑放在炭火上加热，熔化时，金屑成为露滴状，冷却后即成粟粒状的小金珠，最后将小金珠密集地焊接在器物表面，形成所需要的各种图案。炸珠常常和掐丝编织镶嵌一同使用，汉代这种工艺就已经出现，唐代仍很流行，图版27的金筐宝钿团花纹金杯，图版118的金筐宝钿鸿雁纹金梳背就是这种工艺的代表作。

9.焊接

焊接是金银器成型组合及装饰所用工艺之一。金银器的焊接，因焊药的不同而分为锡焊、铜焊和银焊。复杂一些的器物，一般是先将各部分零件分别打作或铸造出来，然后通过焊接将其组合成一体，最后对焊痕做打磨处理，使接缝处光滑无痕。装饰花纹时，也有使用焊接工艺的，如图版8的鎏金海兽水波纹银碗，内心处的海兽纹，就是用银片剪成后焊接在碗心处的。金银器表面用掐丝花结和粟粒金珠作装饰时，采用的则是硬焊法，就是在金器表面与金丝、金珠的接触点上，粘上铜化合物混合粘剂，然后置于炭火上加热，热到100℃时，铜化合物即变成氧化铜，热到600℃时，粘剂炭化，850℃时，炭由氧化铜吸收氧而成为二氧化碳，使金丝、金珠与金器表面接触点上的纯铜析出，890℃时，红铜与金即熔化粘合得天衣无缝了。这种硬焊技术，在汉代就出现了。图版27的金杯和119的金梳背上的金丝、金花装饰也采用的是这种焊接技术。

10.铆接

铆接是金银器成型组合及装饰所用工艺之一。一般在器物的耳、鋬、提梁等附件的衔接处或器身的衔接处，使用铆钉将若干部分固定组合成一体，如图版27金筐宝钿团花纹金杯的鋬就是铆接到杯身处的。河南伊川鸦岭唐齐国太夫人墓出土的“齐国太夫人”提梁银壶，壶体则是由两块银片用银铆钉铆接而成的[99]，方法简便，灵活实用。也有采用铆接方法来装饰花纹的，如图版39的金杯坯，腹部的花纹是用金片剪成后用铆钉固定在其上的。

11.旋切

旋切是金银器整形加工工艺之一。盆、碗、盒、杯等圆形器皿，经捶打成型后，使用旋刀修整其内、外壁，使之平整、光洁。旋刀有多种规格，使用时，先固定中心点，然后按照同一方向快速旋转，所以在盖内面留下针尖大的圆形凹状中心点及密密麻麻等距离的同心圆痕迹。

12.抛光

抛光是金银器整形加工工艺之一。金银器制作成型后，表面较粗糙，光泽度不够明显，一般采用羊肝石、朴炭等先打磨掉粗糙部分，然后使用玛瑙、皮革、头发团等反复擦拭，使器物表面锃亮、圆滑，富有耀眼的光泽。

13.锥刺

锥刺是金银器装饰工艺方法之一。在已经成型的器物表面，用锥子按照事先设计的图案纹饰，刻出连续的圆点，由排列有序的圆点构成纹饰的线条，如图版138的双鹿纹金牌饰，上面的装饰即采取此法，效果古朴、稚拙。

14.错金银

错金银是金银器装饰工艺方法之一。在成型的器物上，用金丝、银丝或金片、银片镶嵌成各种华丽秀美的纹饰或文字，然后用错（厝）石磨错，让金丝、银丝或金片、银片与器物表面光平，最后再经抛光处理，使器表光滑平整，黄白辉映，对比明显，装饰效果很好，如图版1的错金银匜。

15.金银平脱

金银平脱是金银装饰工艺方法之一。将金片（金箔）或银片（银箔）剪成各种花鸟形、人物形，用桐油或鱼鳔胶等将其粘贴在器物表面，然后髹漆数重，再仔细进行碾压、研磨，使金片（金箔）或银片（银箔）的花纹脱露出来与漆面平齐，再加推碾磨光。一般在漆器、铜器的装饰上使用较多，如图版157的四鸾衔绶纹金银平脱铜镜。

四

中国古代金银器不仅工艺复杂、高超，而且造型和装饰也很精巧和细密，可以说是科学与艺术完美结合的佳作。

中国古代金银器从造型上来看，大致有平面的和立体的两种。平面造型，以圆、椭圆、方形、菱形、三角形、六角形等几何形为多见，其次为人物形、植物形以及如意形、云朵形。立体造型可以分为三类：一类是写生的动物形，如虎、豹、羊、狗、鹿、鹰、蛇、啄木鸟以及神灵动物龙、凤、龟等。一类是写生的植物形，如莲花、荷叶、桃、海棠、梅花、柿子、花瓣等。一类是仿物形，仿照生活中常见的物体形象来设计造型，如各种圆、多边的几何体以及蒲篮、蚌壳、月牙甚至楼阁建筑、帆船等。由于观察细腻，比例掌握得准确，体量大者显得稳固、刚劲，小者则显得灵巧、柔和。造型的优美和生动，往往在视觉接触的最初，能先声夺人，留下具有震撼力的印象。

中国古代金银器在花纹图案的装饰上，非常注重整体效果。在安排布局时，有两个明显的特点：一是讲究对称原则，一般是以器物的中轴线为中心，左右相向地布置同样的纹饰，使器物显得均衡和饱满，如图版138、139的金牌饰。二是对比手法运用得非常娴熟，既有大小的对比，高低的对比，动静的对比，又有色彩上的对比，通过对比所形成的各种变化，来突出或强调主题，清晰地表达其文化内涵。如图版30的鎏金胡人乐伎纹八棱银杯，腹部一组乐伎人物主纹全部为高浮雕式，底纹则全部为平地式，以高低起伏来显示其主次关系。图版5的鸳鸯莲瓣纹金碗，腹部视觉最佳位置处被分割成十个小单元，每个小单元的中心，安排的是各不相同的一个动物，或飞禽或走兽，栩栩如生，具有强烈的动感。其下部则以相同的封闭式的忍冬草，营造出十分宁静的气氛，以动静的强烈对比，象征生命的美好和自然的可爱。图版34的鎏金蔓草鸳鸯纹银羽觞，主题纹饰全部鎏金，通过黄白色彩的对比，以醒目的黄色强化了主题。金银器上镶嵌宝石琉璃，则更是以红、绿、蓝色与黄白色所产生的强烈反差，来丰富视觉，增加美感的。

中国古代金银器的装饰，从构图方式上来看，主要有点装和满地装。点装是以个体纹样为单位独立进行重点装饰，其手法简洁大方，效果一目了然。点装又可分为两种：单点式和散点式。单点式是仅仅装饰器物的一点，如图版40的鎏金龟纹桃形银盘。散点式是等距离地反复装饰器物的几个部位，其余留白，如图版20的涂金小簇花纹银盖碗。满地装是以多种纹样对器物通体进行装饰，其手法繁复细密，效果富丽堂皇。满地装主要可以分为5种：一、适合纹样式，根据器物的形态而设计的合适构图；二、连缀纹样式，以流畅的植物枝叶与珍奇动物组成的二方连续图案；三、格律纹样式，由中心旋转45°、60°、120°重复连接相同纹样而组成的八方、六方或三方对称形图案；四、连环画纹样式，在相同的格局内连续出现与同一主题关联的图案；五、装饰画纹样式，整个器物的装饰就是一幅独立而完整的绘画作品，有人物、有风景、有意境。

中国古代金银器的装饰题材极其丰富，从其内容来看，主要有以下7类。

1.植物类

植物类有莲花、蟠桃、牡丹、石榴、葡萄、松枝、菊花、梅花、柿子、西番莲、折枝、缠枝、串枝、忍冬、卷草、佛手、秋葵、玉兰、栀子、桂花、芙蓉、荔枝、香橼以及宝相团花、灵芝、灵果等。先秦至秦汉时，金银器上的植物纹饰种类较少，隋唐开始明显增多，且出现不少外来植物纹样。宋元时期，植物类纹饰仍以写实为主，但明显地增多了南方亚热带植物，并流行瓜果装饰。明清时期，植物类装饰趋于图案化，具有文人画特点的松竹梅组合较为多见。

2.动物类

动物类有啄木鸟、鹰、虎、马、牛、羊、鹿、骆驼、蛇、蝉、鸳鸯、鸿雁、孔雀、鹦鹉、鹤、蝴蝶、蜜蜂、蝙蝠、蝌蚪、兔子、松鼠、狐狸、犀牛、猴子、熊、狮、龟、鲤鱼以及具有神异色彩的龙、凤、飞狮、翼牛、天马、摩羯鱼等。先秦至秦汉时，周边少数民族冠饰、带饰上多用虎、马、鹰等动物装饰，以其形象的勇猛、刚健，来表现少数民族特有的力量和蕴涵。唐代皇室用金银器，流行瑞兽与珍禽纹样，以龙凤、飞狮、天禄、独角兽来象征帝王的神圣、威严和广德，以鸿雁、鸳鸯、孔雀、鹦鹉来象征友情、吉祥、和睦。另外，狐、兔、羊、鹿等狩猎活动中常见的猎物，也多被装饰在器物上，纹饰题材还有着浓重的外来影响。宋元时期，除龙凤外，其他神异动物几乎不见，而小动物明显增多。明清时期的动物纹饰则由自然写实转向呆板的程式化模式。

3.人物故事

人物故事有乐伎、舞伎、家居、狩猎、状元登科、风景人物、神话传说、童子嬉戏、寿星老人等，多为器物的主题纹饰，流行于唐宋元明时期。一般以界栏相隔，以框架的重复出现来反映内容的连贯性。如图版28的鎏金仕女狩猎纹八瓣银杯，杯周身八朵花瓣以柳叶条带作界栏，形成八幅既独立又互相有关联的画面：男子跃马追逐射猎，女子梳妆育婴游乐。宋代科举制度在金银器装饰上也有反映，如福建邵武市故县宋代窖藏出土的一件鎏金银八角杯[100]，外壁八个棱面上装饰出新科状元身着袍服、手执仙桂，骑着骏马，春风得意地在花市中畅游的情景，与内壁杯心处錾刻的《踏莎行》词遥相呼应，充满了诗情画意的时代特色。因器施画，将文人画风格移植于金银器上，这是宋元时期金银器装饰上的一大特点。

4.宗教形象与图案

宗教形象与图案有佛、菩萨、罗汉、飞天、金刚、力士、三钴杵、白象、坐狮、摩尼宝珠、迦陵频嘉鸟、仙鹤、青龙、莲花以及道教的八卦、羽人、真武君等。金银器中最早出现佛教造像的是辽宁北票北燕冯素弗墓出土的金饰片[101]，饰片为山形，中间压印出一佛像，后面有火焰背光，左右各站立一侍从弟子。此饰片似为器物上的附件。唐代出现形美质精的佛教金银造像，如陕西扶风法门寺唐代地宫出土的鎏金珍珠装捧真身菩萨[102]，以金银塑造佛教造像遂成为历代延续的传统。另外，在金棺银椁及佛教使用的法器上，也多以佛、菩萨、罗汉、护法狮子、乐舞伎等作装饰。

5.几何图案

几何图案有圆点、圆圈、三角、菱格、弦纹、辐射线以及变形而成的索套、柳叶条、瓦棱、方胜、联珠、鱼子、云雷等等，一般多用作衬底或作为辅助性装饰，排列方式也多种多样，或上下、左右、斜向地对称式排列，或回旋、抱合、相背地平衡式排列，或一整二破地连续式排列。

6.吉祥图案与文字

中国古代，有以吉祥图案象征美好希望的传统，在金银器上，以龙、凤象征神圣、高贵，以牡丹、宝相花象征荣华富贵，以鹊闹枝头象征喜庆，以鸿雁衔胜象征平安，以石榴鱼子象征人丁兴旺，这在唐代就已经很流行了，只是寓意隐蔽一些，而自然写实的味道更重一些。宋元时期，吉祥图案的用意益加直接明显，如江苏吴县元代吕师孟墓出土的金盘[103]，以四个如意头来象征"事事如意"。明清时期，流行以吉祥图案和吉祥文字来装饰器物，如北京明定陵出土的"福"字银盘，就是直接用单个吉祥字"福"来装饰盘心的。常见的吉祥图案有蝙蝠、如意、戟、磬、鱼、爆竹、花瓶、松竹梅等。吉祥文字则有"福"、"寿"、"喜庆万年"、"祝延万寿"等。常常是以谐声寓意纹样与吉祥文字相组合来表达主题，如爆竹、花瓶与"喜"、"安"相配为喜报平安。

金银器上还有一类非装饰性的题款文字，这种题款文字最早出现于先秦时期。唐代开始，金银器上大多有题款，或朱书，或墨书，或錾刻（有的阴刻后内填朱），或为单线，或为双勾线。题款的内容一般包括年号、制作单位、器物名称、重量、成色、经管官员和工匠的姓名。题款位置一般在器物底部或口沿背面，格式有纵条式、半环式、环式几种。由于是非装饰性文字，一般都弱化处理，决不喧宾夺主。

7.自然景象

自然景象有流云、太阳、月宫、波涛、山岳、海水、江崖等，多作背景或辅助性装饰，如江苏金坛元代窖藏出土的凸花人物故事银盘[104]，湖南通道明代窖藏出土的风景人物画银盘。[105]

金银器上的装饰在安排布局时，常常是多种纹饰交错组合，各种手法巧妙使用，以期取得最佳的装饰效果。而且每个时代的装饰内容和装饰手法，都有着鲜明的时代特色，体现出这个时代特有的文化内涵。

注释

[1] 马克思：《政治经济学批判》，徐坚译，人民出版社，1955年2月第1版。
[2] 文物编辑委员会：《文物考古工作三十年》，文物出版社，1979年11月。
[3] 中国科学院考古研究所：《赤峰药王庙、夏家店遗址试掘简报》，《考古》1961年2期。
[4] 随县擂鼓墩一号墓考古发掘队：《湖北随县曾侯乙墓发掘简报》，《文物》1979年7期。
[5] 司马迁：《史记·孝武本纪》(卷12)，中华书局，1959年9月版。
[6] 陈英英等：《国外学者研究唐代金银器情况介绍》，《考古与文物》1985年2期。
[7] 中国社会科学院考古所等：《定陵》，文物出版社，1990年5月。
[8] 西安市文管会：《西安市东南郊沙坡村出土一批唐代银器》，《文物》1964年6期。
[9] 陕西省博物馆等：《西安南郊何家村发现唐代窖藏文物》，《文物》1972年1期。
[10] 丹徒县文教局等：《江苏丹徒丁卯桥出土唐代银器窖藏》，《文物》1982年11期。
[11] 遂溪县博物馆：《广东遂溪县发现南朝窖藏金银器》，《考古》1986年3期。
[12] 内蒙古文物考古研究所等：《辽陈国公主墓》，文物出版社，1993年4月版。
[13] 陕西省扶风县法门寺考古队：《扶风法门寺塔唐代地宫发掘简报》，《文物》1988年10期。
[14] 安英新：《新疆伊犁昭苏县古墓葬出土金银器等珍贵文物》，《文物》1999年9期。
[15] 马玉基：《大同市小站村花烂塔台北魏墓清理简报》，《文物》1983年8期。
[16] 石家庄文化局文物发掘组：《河北赞皇东魏李希宗墓》，《考古》1977年6期。
[17] 肖梦龙等：《江苏溧阳平桥出土宋代银器窖藏》，《文物》1986年5期。
[18] 吴兴汉：《安徽合肥市区发现一批元朝金银器》，《文物》1956年6期。
[19] 怀化地区文物工作队等：《湖南通道发现南明窖藏银器》，《文物》1984年2期。
[20] 杨伯达：《中国美术全集》(10)，文物出版社，1987年3月版。
[21] 遂溪县博物馆：《广东遂溪县发现南朝窖藏金银器》，《考古》1986年3期。
[22] 出土文物展览工作组编：《文化大革命期间出土文物》(第一辑)，文物出版社，1972年版；孙培良等：《略谈大同市南郊出土的几件银器和铜器》，《文物》1977年9期。
[23] 金柏东等：《浙江永嘉发现窖藏银器》，《文物》1984年5期。
[24] 巴右文等：《内蒙昭乌达盟巴林右旗发现辽代银器窖藏》，《文物》1980年5期。
[25] 陆思贤等：《内蒙古临河县高油房出土的西夏金器》，《文物》1987年11期。
[26] 中国社会科学院考古所等：《定陵》，文物出版社，1990年5月。
[27] 朱家溍：《故宫所藏明清两代有关西藏的文物》，《文物》1959年2期。
[28] 山东省淄博市博物馆：《西汉齐王墓随葬器物坑》，《考古学报》1985年2期。
[29] 夏鼐：《北魏封和突墓出土萨珊银盘考》，《文物》1983年8期；马雍：《北魏封和突墓及其出土的波斯银盘》，《文物》1983年8期。
[30] 初师宾：《甘肃靖远新出东罗马鎏金银盘略考》，《文物》1990年5期。
[31] 宁夏回族自治区博物馆等：《宁夏固原北周李贤夫妇墓发掘简报》，《文物》1985年11期。
[32] 罗丰：《北周李贤墓出土的中亚风格鎏金银瓶》，《考古学报》2000年3期。
[33] 李毓芳：《咸阳市出土一件唐代金壶》，《考古与文物》1982年1期。
[34] 敖汉旗文化馆：《敖汉旗李家营子出土的金银器》，《考古》1978年2期。
[35] 项春松：《赤峰发现的契丹鎏金银器》，《文物》1985年2期。
[36] 张先得等：《北京市郊明武清侯李伟夫妇墓清理简报》，《文物》1979年4期。
[37] 杨伯达：《中国美术全集》(10)，文物出版社，1987年3月版。
[38] 中国社会科学院考古所等：《满城汉墓发掘报告》，文物出版社，1980年10月版。
[39] 丹徒县文教局等：《江苏丹徒丁卯桥出土唐代银器窖藏》，《文物》1982年11期。
[40] 衢州市文管会：《浙江衢州市南宋墓出土器物》，《考古》1983年11期。
[41] 肖梦龙等：《江苏溧阳平桥出土宋代银器窖藏》，《文物》1986年5月。
[42] 中国社会科学院考古所等：《定陵》，文物出版社，1990年5月。
[43] 杨伯达：《中国美术全集》(10)，文物出版社，1987年3月版。
[44] 谢青山等：《山西吕梁县石楼镇又发现铜器》，《文物》1960年7期。
[45] 田广金等：《内蒙古阿鲁柴登发现的匈奴遗物》，《考古》1980年4期。
[46] 陈大为：《辽宁北票房身村晋墓发掘简报》，《考古》1960年1期。
[47] 黎瑶渤：《辽宁北票县西官营子北燕冯素弗墓》，《文物》1973年3期。
[48] 陆思贤等：《达茂旗出土的古代北方民族金饰件》，《文物》1984年1期。
[49] 冯永谦：《辽宁省建平、新民的三座辽墓》，《考古》1960年2期。
[50] 中国社会科学院考古所等：《定陵》，文物出版社，1990年5月。
[51] 张先得等：《北京市郊明武清侯李伟夫妇墓清理简报》，《文物》1979年4期。
[52] 四川省文管会等：《四川平武明王玺家族墓》，《文物》1989年7期。
[53] 中国社会科学院考古所等：《定陵》，文物出版社，1990年5月。
[54] 吉林省文物工作队等：《吉林通榆兴隆山清代公主墓》，《文物》1984年11期。
[55] 苏天钧：《北京西郊小西天清代墓葬发掘简报》，《文物》1963年1期。
[56] 宝鸡市考古工作队：《宝鸡市益门村二号春秋墓发掘简报》，《文物》1993年10期。
[57] 中国科学院考古研究所：《辉县发掘报告》，科学出版社，1956年。
[58] 梁白泉：《国宝大观》，上海文化出版社，1990年8月版。
[59] 云南省博物馆：《云南晋宁石寨山古墓群发掘报告》，文物出版社，1959年3月版。
[60] 郭文魁：《和龙渤海古墓出土的几件金饰》，《文物》1973年8期。
[61] 胡昌钰：《四川什邡县出土金腰带》，《文物》1985年5期。
[62] 靳枫毅：《辽宁朝阳前窗户村辽墓》，《文物》1980年12期。
[63] 内蒙古文物考古研究所等：《辽陈国公主墓》，文物出版社，1993年4月版。
[64] 辽宁省博物馆文物队等：《鞍山倪家台崔源族墓的发掘》，《文物》1978年11期。
[65] 四川省文管会等：《四川平武明王玺家族墓》，《文物》1989年7期。
[66] 中国社会科学院考古所等：《定陵》，文物出版社，1990年5月。
[67] 内蒙古文物考古研究所等：《辽陈国公主墓》，文物出版社，1993年4月版。
[68] 福建省博物馆等：《福州市北郊南宋墓清理简报》，《文物》1997年7期；福建省博物馆：《福州南宋黄昇墓》，文物出版社，1982年3月版；
[69] 江西省博物馆：《江西南城明益王朱祐槟墓发掘简报》，《文物》1973年7期。
[70] 中国社会科学院考古所等：《定陵》，文物出版社，1990年5月版。
[71] 林士民：《浙江宁波天封塔地宫发掘报告》，《文物》1991年6期。
[72] 陆思贤等：《内蒙古临河县高油房出土的西夏金器》，《文物》1987年11期。

[73] 河北省文物研究所等：《河北固安于沿村金宝严寺塔基地宫出土文物》，《文物》1993年4期。
[74] 金甲：《中国历代纪年佛像图典》，文物出版社，1994年6月版。
[75] 临潼县博物馆：《临潼唐庆山寺舍利塔基精室清理记》，《文物》1985年5期。
[76] 陕西省扶风县法门寺考古队：《扶风法门寺塔唐代地宫发掘简报》，《文物》1988年10期。
[77] 河南省古代建筑保护研究所等：《河南邓州市福胜寺塔地宫》，《文物》1991年6期。
[78] 陕西省扶风县法门寺考古队：《扶风法门寺塔唐代地宫发掘简报》，《文物》1988年10期。
[79] 大理州文管所等：《下关市佛图塔实测和清理报告》，《文物》1986年7期。
[80] 刘友恒等：《河北正定天宁寺凌霄塔地宫出土文物》，《文物》1991年6期。
[81] 陕西省扶风县法门寺考古队：《扶风法门寺塔唐代地宫发掘简报》，《文物》1988年10期。
[82] 齐心等：《北京房山县北郑村辽塔清理记》，《考古》1980年2期。
[83] 定县博物馆：《河北定县发现两座宋代塔基》，《文物》1972年8期。
[84] 林士民：《浙江宁波天封塔地宫发掘报告》，《文物》1991年6期。
[85] 河北省文物研究所等：《河北固安于沿村金宝严寺塔基地宫出土文物》，《文物》1993年4期。
[86] 中国社会科学院考古所等：《满城汉墓发掘报告》，文物出版社，1980年10月版。
[87] 宁夏固原博物馆：《宁夏固原唐史道德墓清理简报》，《文物》1985年11期。
[88] 内蒙古文物考古研究所等：《辽陈国公主墓》，文物出版社，1993年4月版。
[89] 衢州市文管会：《浙江衢州市南宋墓出土器物》，《考古》1983年11期。
[90] 江西省文物考古所等：《江西德安南宋周氏墓清理简报》，《文物》1990年9期。
[91] 巴林右旗文化馆：《内蒙古巴林右旗出土金银葬具》，《文物》1995年1期。
[92] 四川省博物馆等：《明兵部尚书赵炳然夫妇合葬墓》，《文物》1982年2期。
[93] 中国社会科学院考古所等：《定陵》，文物出版社，1990年5月。
[94] 江西省文物工作队：《江西南城明益定王朱由木墓发掘简报》，《文物》1983年2期。
[95] 甘肃省博物馆：《兰州市上西园村明墓清理简报》，《考古》1960年3期。
[96] 姚迁：《江苏南窑庄楚汉文物窖藏》，《文物》1982年11期。
[97] 云南省文物工作队：《大理崇圣寺三塔主塔的实测和清理》，《考古学报》1981年2期。
[98] 陕西省博物馆等：《西安南郊何家村发现唐代窖藏文物》，《文物》1972年1期。
[99] 洛阳市第二文物工作队：《伊川鸦岭唐齐国太夫人墓》，《文物》1995年11期。
[100] 王振镛等：《邵武故县发现一批宋代银器》，《福建文博》1982年1期。
[101] 黎瑶渤：《辽宁北票县西官营子北燕冯素弗墓》，《文物》1973年3期。
[102] 陕西省扶风县法门寺考古队：《扶风法门寺塔唐代地宫发掘简报》，《文物》1988年10期。
[103] 江苏省文管会：《江苏吴县元墓清理简报》，《文物》1959年11期。
[104] 肖梦龙：《江苏金坛元代青花云龙罐窖藏》，《文物》1980年11期。
[105] 怀化地区文物工作队等：《湖南通道发现南明窖藏银器》，《文物》1984年2期。

参考书目：

陆九皋、韩伟：《唐代金银器》，文物出版社，1985年版。
韩伟：《海内外唐代金银器萃编》，三秦出版社，1989年版。
齐东方：《唐代金银器研究》，中国社会科学出版社，1999年版。
盖瑞忠：《隋唐工艺史》，台湾省立博物馆印行。

Shen Qinyan

Brief Introduction to the Gold and Silver Wares of Ancient China

I

Gold and silver have been particularly appreciated and treasured by human beings from early times for their physical attributes: beautiful colors, soft luster, optical effect and don't corrode, rust or fade, even more, they can be easily worked into any forms of ornaments. In ancient China, gold and silver weres associated with the concepts of longevity and immortality. And they were regarded as the symbols of social status, power, wealth and virtue. Daoist tried to confer the enduring qualities of gold to human soul because they believed gold could create an effect of stabilizing soul and lengthening life. Gold and silver weres not only highly valued as precious items in one's lifetime, but also as the luxurious burial objects which were contemplated as the continuation of secular life in the nether world.

The term of gold and silver can be used in a broad and a narrow sense. In the broad sense, they refer to all objects related to the metals of gold and silver, while in the narrow sense, they are limited to those made of gold and silver. Most of the surviving gold and silver wares were from the archaeological excavations. It has been proved that the earliest appearance of gold and silver works was approximately at the Xia dynasty (2,070 ~ 1,600 B.C.). Towards the Spring and Autumn period, gold and silver were extensively used for the purpose of surface decoration as inlays or coatings on wood, bronze and lacquers, as well as the personal ornaments such as bracelets, armlets, earrings and head accessories. The earliest examples of gold vessels, dating to the sixth or fifth century B.C., are five gold items unearthed from the tomb of the Marquis Yi of Zeng, who died about 433B.C., altogether with the garment hooks and appliques in gold. Among which, a gold cup is of particular importance. It weighs 2.15 kg and is made of 98% pure gold. Afterwards, gold was cast into ornaments and adjuncts to other metals, such as weapons, jewellery and burial items. In the Qin dynasty, gold and silver were used to embellish the reins or chariots. This fact is exemplified by the 747 pieces of gold and 817 pieces of silver ornaments found on the horse decoration and in the manufacture of soul chariots for Emperor Qin Shihuang, which displayed the great achievement the Qin metalworkers had reached in the making of gold and silver. By the Han dynasty gold and silver were becoming more and more important, and the gilding of silver and bronze had also being practiced. The Han emperors had a special interest in gold, they always rewarded the court officials with gold foil. Conversely, the gold and silver wares were also considered very prestigious and acceptable gifts to be given to emperors by the officials at different levels in order to gain favor from emperors. During the Wei, Jin, Northern and Southern dynasties, the foreign gold and silver wares were imported in a large scale with the frequent invasions of non-Chinese peoples and the introduction and consolidation of Buddhism, which had great influence on the Chinese traditional metal industry. This influence increased rapidly until the great Tang dynasty when more exotic items flooded in. Based upon the absorption, imitation and infusion of foreign elements, the Chinese artisans created a native style of metal works through the indigenous interpretation of Western classical designs, which showed a fresh, colorful, sophisticated and elegant flavor. In the Song dynasty, the provincial and private manufacturing of gold and silver were running wild, the products were characterized by the marks of workshops or artisans and introduction of the paintings as the new motif. The Liao dynasty was established by the horse-riding minority called Khitan for whom the gold and silver had played a very important role in their nomadic life. Full of national traits, the Liao wares became the focus of the world attention such as the cock-peak-shaped ewer and handled pot etc. During the Yuan, Ming and Qing dynasties, the techniques of gem settings or pearl inlaying was greatly developed, by which the objects looked more practical and attractive.

Generally, there were two sources for the gold and silver wares. One was handed down from ancient times, mainly descended from the imperial family of the Qing dynasty, but the number is rather small. Another was from the archaeological excavations, and the majority of them were from hoards and crypts, whereas the tombs scarcely yielded such items. Since 1949, more than 10,000 pieces of gold and silver objects had been unearthed from the remains of 170 old cities all around China, dating from the Xia dynasty down to the Qing dynasty. These findings are in a wide variety, and provide a lot of information about the contemporary social life including economy, politics, military, religions, arts and handicraft technology. As the capitals of thirteen dynasties, Shaanxi had always been the cultural and diplomatic center for over 1,000 years. Xi'an, the east terminal of the Silk Road, was the assembly center of the exotic goods, included gold and silver which soon became a necessity for Chinese elite. The ancient tombs, hoards and Buddhism crypts in Shaanxi province had revealed more than 20 groups of gold and silver wares, comprising half percent of the total in China. Among them, the most important discoveries include the Shapo village hoard, the Hejiacun village hoard and the Famen Temple crypt, they represent the three stages of the development of the Tang gold and silver making: early, middle and late. The early period was called foreign-inspired time when the foreign-looking objects were very current, such as a Sogdian style bowl from Shapo hoard. The decoration is characterized by the geometrical and formal rigidity, which was popular in the Near Eastern designs, the intricate flowers and hunting scenes against a ring punched background. The second period (probably the second half of the eighth century) was the Chinese adaptation and combination of foreign elements with the local taste. The 271 pieces of gold and silver wares from Hejiacun illustrated that an indigenous style was formative, although the foreign influence was still so prevalent. The decoration motif included centrally placed creatures surrounded by flowers against a plain silver background. The third phase (the mid-ninth century) was purely Chinese. Hundreds of the Buddhism utensils contained in the deposit of the Famen Temple were the most typical examples, such as the eared wine cups with design of large floral sprays against decorated or undecorated background, but the patterns are less tightly worked than those of the earlier period. The items from Yaoxian dated between 849～851 are also typical.

II

According to their functions, gold and silver wares can be divided into nine sorts: daily utensils, dress ornaments, religious images and reliquaries, burial objects, animal-shaped ornaments, medical vessels, jewellery, chariot and horse decoration, coins and tools etc. The former six sorts are commonly seen while the others are rarely found. Besides, there are few kinds of less found such as sacrificial objects, weapons and models, but scarcely survived.

1.Daily Utensils Daily utensil occupies the largest proportion and played an important role in the daily life of the upper class. It consists of food vessels (cups, stemmed cup, dish, bowl, pot, tripod, ewer and ladle etc), containers (jar, box, bottles for medicines and religious ceremonies), household wares (vase, lamp, incense burner, mirror stand, perfumer). Cups are one of the earliest gold and silver vessels in ancient China. Around the fourth century B.C., the King of Chu State already used gold cups as drinking vessels, it probably was the earliest piece. From the Northern dynasty down to the Tang dynasty, foreign cups were imported into China along the Silk Road which enriched the style and decoration of their local kinds. The cups of this period were shaped as flowers, leaves, octagons, hexagons and ovals as well as stemmed-cups, waisted cups, foliage or lobed cups and carinated cups etc. Bowl wasn't manufactured until the Northern and Southern dynasties under the foreign influence.

More than 60 bowls were uncovered from Hejiacun hoard, of which some are exotic style and some are indigenous flavor such as round, floral, petals and the imitation of folk basket etc. After the Tang dynasty, the bowl making was still popular. Many exquisite examples were revealed from the remains of this period, including the decorated bowls of the Song dynasty from Yongjia county of Zhejiang province, an eight-petalled silver bowl dating to the Liao dynasty from Balinyouqi at Zhaowudameng in Inner Mongolia, a gold bowl of the Western Xia dynasty embellished with phoenix design from the old city remains of Gaoyoufang in Linhe county, Inner Mongolia, and a silver bowl of the Ming dynasty with peony designs from the Dingling mausoleum in Beijing etc. The earliest dish, also the only discovery of the Qin dynasty dish, was from a satellite tomb of the Western Han dynasty at Wotuo village, Linzi county of Shandong province. In the Tang dynasty, the dish making reached its apex time both in style and design, and many new shapes were created either circular on three feet or highly lobed and indented in outline. The rims varied as rhombus, petals, cut-open peach and lotus etc, and the base as flat, flared, ring, trumpet, everted, three-footed or four-footed. The most striking ewer was found at a Northern Zhou tomb in Guyuan, Ningxia. It was silver with gilding, and shaped with a tall and slender neck, pear-shaped body and high beaded foot. The beading design and the figures in diaphanous dresses were certainly of foreign origin. Gold basin is rarely seen, the two pieces from Hejiacun are the only surviving examples of its kinds in China. It has been proved that such gold basins were used for ceremonial ablutions, and might belong in the royal households. When a prince or princess was born, he or she was given a ceremonial washing in a gold basin. The biggest basin is gilded silver one from the crypt of the Famen Temple, its rim diameter is about 46 cm, and decorated with mandarin ducks and floral medallions. However, the gold basin was hardly found after the Tang dynasty.

2. **Dress Ornaments** Gold and silver wares used as jewellery, belt sets and swings, and hanging pendants in ancient China. From an early date in Chinese history, men wore girdles to hold up their trousers or fasten the robes. Since the Spring and Autumn period, the belt hook became a common male accessory and a large number have been found in the Eastern Zhou tombs. With the frequent contacts between the Han people and the riding tribes in the north border of China, the using and making of belt hook became very popular. Many were very richly inlaid with jade, glass, silver and gold, all markers of social status and wealth. Jewellery consists of five types: hat ornaments, hairpins, necklace, earrings, bracelets and rings. Hairpins originated in the Neolithic Age and were used by both man and women. There are two types of hairpins: one has two parallel prongs of equal length, and the other has only one prong, undecorated or decorated and top gilded or with molded and engraved decoration. The earliest hairpin was discovered at a Shang dynasty tomb in Pinggu of Beijing. During the Wei, Jin, Northern and Southern dynarties, gold and silver hair decorations were extensively used. Towards the Sui and Tang dynasties, it was fashionable for the women's hairs to be dressed higher and higher in chignons and false buns, which necessitated the use of hairpins. Furthermore, the hairpins were considered as the indicators of one's status and were amongst the ornaments listed in the laws of the first Tang Emperor: the lower down the social hierarchy one belonged, the fewer hairpins one was allowed to wear. During the Song and Ming dynasties, the making of hairpins reached the zenith period in style and decoration. The designs included images, flowers, birds and beasts as well as the auspicious symbols. Belt decoration comprises of belt set, belt plaques and belt hooks. The earliest belt hook was made of jade, and a number of examples were unearthed from the remains of Liangzhu Culture (3,300 ~ 2,200 B.C.). Around the Eastern Zhou period, metal-made belt hook became a common male accessory and a large number have been found at the tombs of this period. Gold and silver hooks were not only used as the attachments to the belts, but also as the indicators of wealth and rank. After the Han dynasty, gold and silver hooks were replaced by the belt sets or plaques, also the distinct symbols of upper class. Belt plaques were introduced from the Ordos tribes who particularly skilled at the making of animal-style plaques. The Chinese versions of the Ordos style plaques have been found in a large area spanning from north to south. Belt set consists of several plaques and a rounded buckle, such as that found at the tombs of the Liao dynasty in Inner Mongolia and Liaoning province. In the early Tang dynasty, the belt plaques were made in diversified shapes whereas most of the plaques in the later Tang were approximately square with generally one or two sections of an extended oblong shape, with one rounded and one straight end. There was strict limits for the use of plaques by the imperial law such as civil and military officials of third rank

and above wore thirteen pieces, those of the fourth down to the eighth ranks wore eleven, ten, nine and eight pieces respectively. Belt with gold and jade swings were the unique items of Khitan minority. The representative discoveries included: a gilded silver belt with engraved designs from the tomb of Cui Sheng at Anshan of Liaoning province, gold belt plaques from the tomb of Wang Xi in Pingwu, Sicuan province and the pear-inlaid gold belt sets from the Dingling mausoleum in Beijing.

3. **Religious Objects** The majority of the gold and silver religious objects belonged to the deposits in the Buddhism crypts. But the vessels of Taoism and other cults were scarcely found. The Buddhism objects included images, reliquaries and ritual objects. The earliest Buddhism image was the gold one from the tomb of Feng Sufu of the Northern Yan period, in Beipiao county, Liaoning province. At this period, more and more Chinese people adopted Buddhism and became the devout followers, and the gilded bronze Buddhism images were very popular. In the great Tang dynasty, Buddhism developed into a pure Chinese religion and the gold and silver images were particularly rich. Used as the containers for holding the sarira of Buddha, the reliquaries were considered the most holy offerings to Sakyamuni, including jar, bottle, casket, cabinet and coffin etc. Most of them were decorated with the symbolic designs of Buddhism such as lotus, *baoxiang* medallions, Bodhisattvas and flying apsaras. The ceremonial objects consists of alms bowl, ewer, *Ruyi* lappet (S-shaped ornamental object, a symbol of good luck), holy vase, vajras, wheel of the law etc. The largest hoard of Buddhism items were from the Famen Temple and the most important objects were the sets of caskets, one of which is believed to hold the figure bone of Buddha. The gold staff with twelve small rings and the pure gold basin were also regarded as the masterpieces of the metalworking of the Tang dynasty. Other similar objects included a silver vajras of Fengyou reign of the Southern Zhao period from Xiayuan County of Yunnan province, a gilded silver ewer of the Song dynasty from the basement of the Lingxiao Pagoda at the Tianning temple in Zhengding county of Hebei province. The certain kinds of offerings included caskets, Bodhisattva, incense burners, lamps, tea sets, flowers, Mani-pearls, plaques and banners etc. Among which, the most valuable pieces are five sets of gold and silver caskets and the items used for preparing tea, such as the wheel and the stand for grinding tea and a tea sieve.

4. **Burial Objects** Burial objects can be divided into corpse fittings, masks, stoves and coins etc. The most famous corpse cover was a set of jade garment woven with gold wire from a Western Han tomb of Liusheng in Mancheng, Hebei province. The gold mask from the Tang tomb of Shi Daode in Guyuan, Ningxia, is the only find of its kind in China. The Khitan minority had a burial custom of interring the dead with quantities of gold and silver objects. Numbers of beautiful items such as the gilded silver crown, gold mask, silver pillow and boots with gilded patterns were buried in the tomb of Princess Chengguo at Zelimu, Inner Mongolia. Coins were the often seen as burials in the tombs of the Sui, Tang, Ming and Qing dynasties. But others like silver figurines, silver sticks and gold or silver stoves are rarely discovered.

III

The manufacturing of Chinese gold and silver wares belonged to the techniques of bronze casting before the introduction of Western objects. The skills of shaping and decorating metal vessels are the methods of universal gold and silver smithing, such as hammering, punching, mold casting, repousse and chasing, granulation, fire gilding, openwork, filigree wires, soldering, piercing, gold and silver inlays, gold and silver mounting, riveting and polishing etc.

1. **Repousse and Chasing** A technique of working sheet metal from the reverse side with punches to raise the pattern, which stands in relief on the front. In repousse, the sheet gold was formed on elastic bed of pitch or wood with a hammer and a punch to create sculptural relief. The details were added on the obverse side by chasing (also means tracing). This process was always done by using a tool with a rounded end, such as a hammer or a blunt-ended punch.

2. **Granulation** An important design element for lines and surface decoration by soldering minute grains of gold (granules) to the background, but the solder has always been invisible. Gold granules, only a fraction of a millimeter in diameter, were produced by three methods. The first method was pouring molten gold into water, or onto a smooth stone lying in water, then the drop-like grains resulted. In the second method, molten gold was poured into charcoal dust, and spherical granules were produced. For the third method, gold dust was melted and rotated with charcoal dust in a crucible to form spheres. The technique of arranging single granules

in lines or hammering wire into a grove with hemispherical depressions called beading. And the method for fixing the gold granules on the base surface was called colloidal fusion welding. Mixing the powdered copper carbonate or pulverized malachite with a bonding agent such as fish glue, then heat the mixture to 890℃, when the bonding agent evaporated, only the copper and gold alloy was left. Finally, a nearly invisible, permanent bond between the granules and base surface formed.

3. Filigree An ornamentation technique of fine wires forming an intricate, open design either soldered to a background or left as openwork. First, using a chisel to cut fine strips from sheet metal, and then wrapping the thin gold strips into a spiral, which was drawn out lengthwise and hammered to the desired thinness. The spiral ridges along the longitudinal axis of the wire could be seen under a microscope.

4. Soldering A method of joining two metal surface using an alloy with a lower melting point. This method was generally done with inorganic copper compounds, for example, pulverized copper ore such as malachite (carbonate of copper). These materials were then applied to the surface of gold with organic bonding agent such as fish glue. When fired in a charcoal oven, the glue carbonized and copper carbonate was converted into copper oxide at 100℃. At 600 ℃, the bonding agent was completely carbonized and at 850 ℃, the copper oxide gave off the oxygen (reduction). The carbon dioxide, which was formed by the oxygen compounded with the carbonized bonding agent, evaporated. Traces of pure copper remained which alloyed with the gold at 890℃. This gold or copper alloy had a lower melting point than either of the pure metals, gold (1063℃) and copper (1083℃), so that the materials were jointed on the contact surface by fusion without being melted themselves.

5. Fire Gilding The process for applying gold to the surface of an object made from another material. Gold dust was triturated with warmed mercury to a pasty amalgam, and the mixture was brushed to the object to be gilded—— usually this was made of silver, copper or brass. When the object was heated, the mercury evaporated and the gold or silver remained on the surface as a matted platting layer, which was then burnished. Fire gilding by this method was first described in the first century by Plinius (Natural History, Vol.33) and Vitruvius (On Architecture, Vol. 7). The Egyptians used lead instead of mercury.

6. Casting A traditional technique for making bronze in China which comprised of three methods: open mold casting, massive casting and lost wax process (cire perdue). In the open mold casting, the desired form was carved into a stone or pressed into clay and molten metal was poured into the hollow. For the casting in the round, the interlocking projects were used to align the mold parts and to prevent shifting during casting. For massive casting, the entire form was filled with metal, whereas for hollow objects, a clay core, held in place by small connecting pegs, almost filled the mold, leaving only a thin, hollow space, which was then filled with molten metal. In the lost wax process, a prototype of the desired figure was carved in wax and then encased (invested) in clay, leaving the funnel—shaped spruce and air vents open. When the clay was fired, the wax melted and ran out. The resulted hollow form was filled through the spruce with molten metal, and when it solidified, the mold was smashed. When extra, negative forms were made of carved wax figure, the prototype could be preserved and reused for multiple copies.

7. Ring Matting or Ring Punching A surface decoration on form of matting. It was produced by means of a tool with a concave circular tip, resulting in an overall pattern of small indented circles. Sometimes a tool with more than one ring was used.

8. Openwork Any variety of open pattern, such as one formed by cutting out portions of metal with a chisel. It was mostly used in the decoration of incense burner, perfumer and hairpins.

9. *Pingtuo* Technique A traditional method for decorating the lacquer and bronze wares. Thin sheets of gold and silver were cut out to the desired forms of flowers, birds or figures, and were inlayed into a smooth lacquer surface with attaching agents such as fish glue or tung oil. Then punch the surface over and over in order to make the inlays flatten with the lacquer. This method was popular during Xuanzong's reign but was forbidden by Emperor Suzong (r. 756～72) as too costly after the devastation of the country during An Lushan's rebellion. The process was similar to the western technique called niello, a black compound of silver, lead, copper and sulphur applied to the metal, in the manner of enamel.

IV

The making of gold and silver was a perfect combination

of science and art. Quantities of archaeological finds illustrated how the Chinese developed a series of indigenous skills of shaping and decorating the metal works. The gold and silver wares include two kinds of shapes: plane style and cubist style. The plane shape is often seen as round, oval, square, rhombus, triangle, hexagonal as well as foliate, *Ruyi* cloud-head and figures etc. The cubist shape consists of three parts: animals, plants and object imitations. Animals include tiger, goat, dog, deer, eagle, snake, woodpecker and panther, and the divine creatures like dragon, phoenix and turtle entwining with snake etc. Plants comprise of lotus, peach, persimmon, Chinese-flowering- crabapple, plum blossom and petals etc. The object imitation has such shapes as basket, mussel shell, crescent moon, pavilion, circular or multi-edged stereoscopic etc.

The ancient Chinese placed a particular emphasis on the overall effect of decoration. The artisans had a clever use of systematic composition and balance principle. In the systematic composition, the designs were arranged on the two sides of the axis by which an effect of rhythm and proportion was produced. The balance principle was depicted in the sharp contrast with big and small, high and short, motion and motionless, deep color and light color, dense and sparse etc. Changes were created, the theme was emphasized and the cultural context was clearly expressed.

There were two methods for surface decoration: dotted layout and all-the-surface distribution. In the dotted decoration, a single pattern was stressed, and thus resulted a clean, simple but conspicuous effect. This method was expressed in two ways: single dot and scatter dots. The single dot was arranged at certain part of a vessel, while the scatter dots were interspersed regularly on the surface, such as continuous pattern, serial pictures, scenes in the cartouches, alternative groups, punctuating panels and independent pattern etc.

The decorative motifs on the gold and silver are very rich, including plants, animals, historical stories, religious images and patterns, geometric forms, auspicious creatures and characters, and the scenes from nature etc. Plants include lotus, peach, peony, pomegranate, grapes, pine branch, plum blossom, persimmon, floral sprays, chrysanthemum, flower strings, acanthus, vine scrolls, honeysuckle, trailing flower scrolls, fingered citron, sunflower, lichee, cottonrose hibiscus, cape jasmine, waterchestnut flowers, *Yulan* magnolia and floral medallions etc. Animals include woodpecker, eagle, horse, cow, goat, deer, camel, snake, cicada, mandarin duck, peacock, parrot, butterfly, wagtail, rhinoceros, wild goose, lion, bear, turtle, fox as well as the fantastical creatures like dragon, phoenix, flying lion, winged cow, flying horse, unicorn, Makara etc. All of them were respected as the symbols of majesty, virility, virtue, friendship, auspices and harmony. The figures and stories portrayed the human life such as musicians, dancers, hunting scenes, fairy tales, legend, the top successful candidats in imperial examination, children at playing, and the longevity elderly etc. Most of them belonged to the theme motifs and were framed by panels in the later dynasties, which provide a panorama of the serial scenes. Religious images and patterns described Buddha, Bodhisattva, arhat, flying apsaras, heavenly god, vajra, elephant, seated lion, Mani pearl, Kalavinka birds, blue dragon, lotus and white crane as well as the Eight Diagrams, immortals and winged deities. Geometric forms consist of circle, triangle, rhombus, strings, stylized rope knots, willow leaf, tile-ridge, beads and dots. They were mostly designed as the background or accessory decoration. Auspicious patterns and characters were used to show people's good feelings and pursuits towards the happy life. So certain kinds of animals and plants were given some metaphorical meanings, for example, dragon and phoenix symbolized majesty and superiority, peony and lotus medallion depicted wealth and good fortune, magpies and bunches of flowers indicated happiness and celebration, wild goose holding ribbon in its mouth contained safety and peace, pomegranate and fish rendered the growing families etc. Natural scenes were the sketches of the real world such as the floating cloud, sun, moon palace, waves, mountains and seawaters, also used as the background or supplementary designs.

The decoration on a gold or silver always incorporated several design elements and metal skills in order to create the best effect. The decorative methods and patterns vividly reflect the distinct features of the time spirit and the aesthetic trend of the nobility.

图版

PLATES

1 错金银匜　西汉
Yi, a pouring vessel. Western Han dynasty.

2 鎏金鸿雁衔绶纹银匜　唐
Yi, a pouring vessel. Tang dynasty.

3 鎏金鸳鸯鸿雁纹银匜　唐
Yi, a pouring vessel. Tang dynasty.

4 素面大银盆　唐
Basin. Tang dynasty.

5A 鸳鸯莲瓣纹金碗　唐
Bowl with design of mandarin ducks and lotus petals. Tang dynasty.

5B 内底
The interior side of the bowl.

5C 外底
The exterior side of the bowl.

6 鸳鸯莲瓣纹金碗　唐
Bowl with design of mandarin ducks and lotus petals. Tang dynasty.

7 赤金盆　唐
Basin. Tang dynasty.

8A 鎏金海兽水波纹银碗　唐
Bowl with design of sea animals and waves. Tang dynasty.

8B 内底
The interior side of the bowl.

8C 外底
The exterior side of the bowl

9A 鎏金双狮衔枝纹银碗　唐
Bowl with design of two lions holding floral sprays in their mouths. Tang dynasty.

9B 内底
The interior side of the bowl

10A 鎏金双鱼纹银碗　唐
Bowl with design of two fish. Tang dynasty.

10B 内底
The interior side of the bowl.

11 鎏金花鸟纹银碗　唐
Bowl with design of flowers and birds. Tang dynasty.

12 鎏金花鸟纹银碗　唐
Bowl with design of flowers and birds. Tang dynasty.

13A 鎏金蔓草龙凤纹银碗　唐
Bowl with design of dragon, phoenix and vine scrolls. Tang dynasty.

13B 外底
The exterior side of the bowl

14 素面金碗　唐
Bowl. Tang dynasty.

15 素面卵形银碗　唐
Bowl. Tang dynasty.

16 素面银碗　唐

Bowl. Tang dynasty.

17 素面银碗　唐

Bowl. Tang dynasty.

18A 素面银碗　唐
Bowl. Tang dynasty.

18B 内底墨书
The ink characters on the interior side of the bowl

19 鎏金折枝花纹银盖碗　唐
Lidded bowl with design of floral sprays. Tang dynasty.

20A 鎏金小簇花纹银盖碗　唐
Lidded bowl with design of floral clusters. Tang dynasty.

20B 内底墨书
The ink characters on the interior side of the bowl

21 鎏金宝相花纹银盖碗　唐
Lidded bowl with design of floral medallions. Tang dynasty.

22 鎏金鱼纹银碗　唐
Bowl with design of fish. Tang dynasty.

23 鎏金鸿雁纹四曲银碗　唐
Four-lobed bowl with design of wild geese. Tang dynasty.

24A “宣徽酒坊”银碗　唐
Bowl with inscription of "*xuan hui jiu fang*". Tang dynasty.

24B 外底
The exterior side of the bowl

25 鎏金蔓草花鸟纹高足银杯　唐
High-footed cup with design of flowers, birds and vine scrolls. Tang dynasty.

26 狩猎纹高足银杯　唐
High-footed cup with design of hunting scene. Tang dynasty.

27 金筐宝钿团花纹金杯　唐
Cup with filigree design of stylized flower medallions. Tang dynasty.

28A 鎏金仕女狩猎纹八瓣银杯　唐
Octagonal-shaped cup with design of ladies and hunting scene. Tang dynasty.

28B 外底
The exterior side of the cup

29 伎乐纹八棱金杯　唐
Octagonal-shaped cup with design of musicians. Tang dynasty.

30A 鎏金胡人伎乐纹八棱银杯　唐
Octagonal-shaped cup with design of musicians. Tang dynasty.

30B 杯身外壁
The exterior wall of the cup.

30C 杯身外壁
The exterior wall of the cup

31A 人物纹八棱金杯　唐
Octagonal-shaped cup with design of figures. Tang dynasty.

31B 杯身外壁
The exterior wall of the cup

32 鎏金蔓草纹八棱银杯　唐
Octagonal-shaped cup with design of vine scrolls. Tang dynasty.

33 素面单环柄银杯　唐
Water vessel with single-ringed handle. Tang dynasty.

34 鎏金蔓草鸳鸯纹银羽觞(2件) 唐
Cups with design of mandarin ducks and vine scrolls (2 pieces). Tang dynasty.

35 鎏金摩羯纹银长杯 唐
Cup with design of Makara. Tang dynasty.

36A 摩羯纹金长杯　唐
Cup with design of Makara. Tang dynasty.

36B 内底
The interior side of the cup.

37 五曲高足银杯　唐
Five-lobed and high-footed cup. Tang dynasty.

38 金杯坯　唐
Semi-finished cup. Tang dynasty.

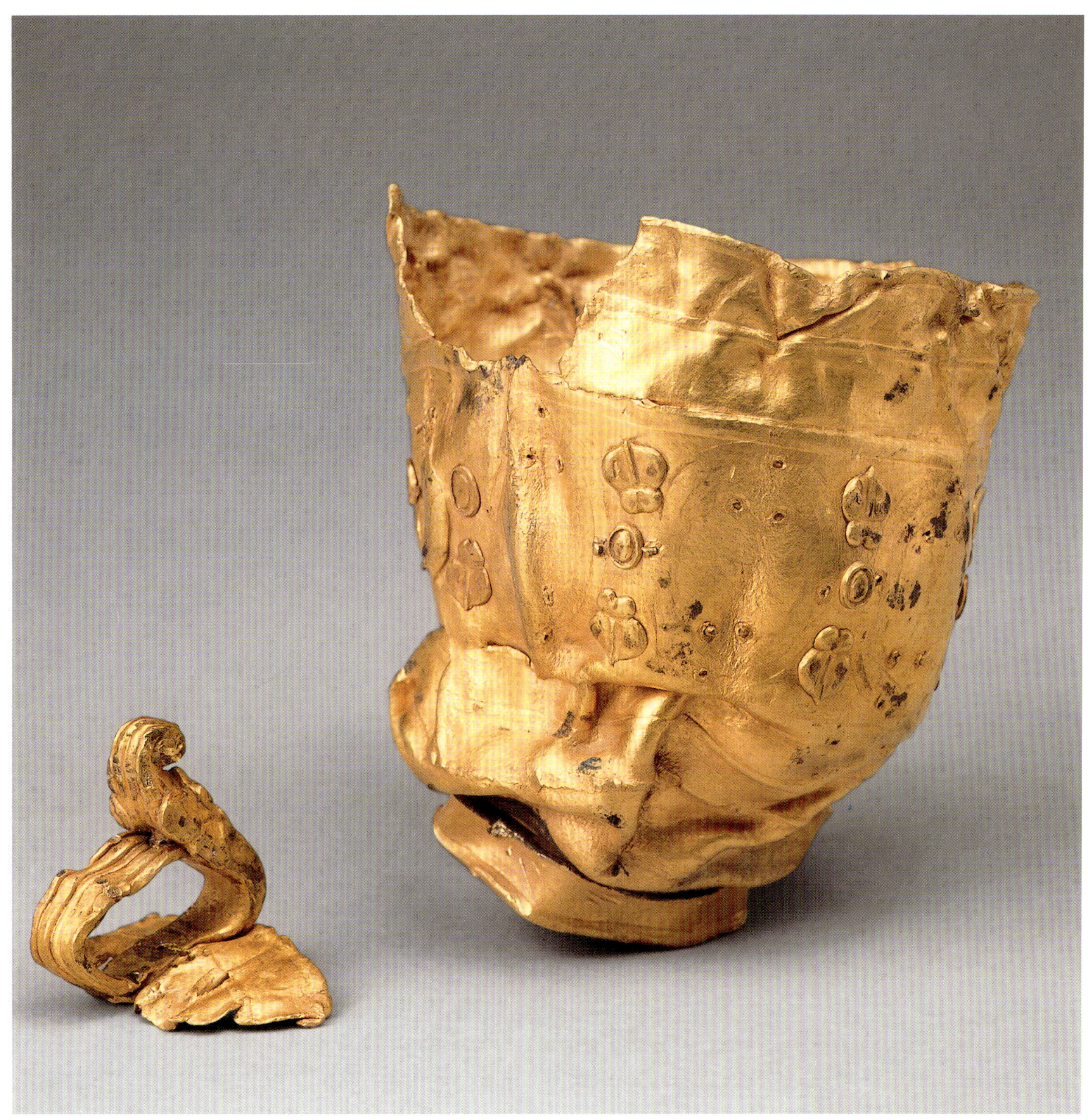

39 金杯坯 唐
Semi-finished cup. Tang dynasty.

40 鎏金龟纹桃形银盘　唐
Cut-peach-shaped dish with design of a turtle. Tang dynasty.

41 鎏金双狐纹双桃形银盘　唐
Double-peach-shaped dish with design of two foxes. Tang dynasty.

42 鎏金熊纹六曲银盘　唐
Six-lobed dish with design of a bear. Tang dynasty.

43 鎏金飞廉纹六曲银盘　唐
Six-lobed dish with design of a phoenix-looking bird. Tang dynasty.

44 鎏金鸾鸟纹六曲银盘　唐
Six-lobed dish with design of a phoenix. Tang dynasty.

45 鎏金“裴肃进”双凤纹六曲银盘　唐
Dish with design of two phoenixes. Tang dynasty.

46 鎏金凤鸟纹葵形大银盘(残) 唐
Dish with design of a phoenix (fragment). Tang dynasty.

47 鎏金“敬晦进”折枝团花纹五曲银碟 唐
Dish with inscription of "*jing hui jin*". Tang dynasty.

48A 鎏金鸿雁纹四曲银碟　唐
Four-lobed dish with design of wild geese. Tang dynasty.

48B 内底
The interior side of the dish

49 五曲葵口银碟　唐
Five-lobed and sunflower-rimmed dish. Tang dynasty.

50 莲瓣形银茶托　唐
Lotus-petal-shaped tea cup stand. Tang dynasty.

51 鎏金双鱼纹四曲银碟　唐
Four-lobed dish with design of two fish. Tang dynasty.

52 素面五尖瓣形银碟　唐
Five-petal-shaped dish. Tang dynasty.

53 素面海棠形银碟　唐
Chinese-flowering-crabapple-shaped dish. Tang dynasty.

54 鎏金“李杆进”鸳鸯绶带纹五曲银碟　唐
Dish with inscription of "*li gan jin*". Tang dynasty.

55 鎏金折枝花纹五曲银碟　唐
Dish with design of floral sprays. Tang dynasty.

56 双耳提梁银锅　唐
Pot with two ears and an arc handle. Tang dynasty.

57 双耳提梁银锅 唐

Pot with two ears and an arc handle. Tang dynasty.

58 双耳银锅　唐

Pot with two ear handles. Tang dynasty.

59 花叶形单柄银铛　唐

Handled medicine warmer with three leaf-shaped feet. Tang dynasty.

60A 金药铫　唐
Medicine warmer. Tang dynasty.

60B 内底墨书
Ink characters on the interior side of the warmer

61A 双狮纹金铛　唐
Medicine warmer with design of two lions. Tang dynasty.

61B 内底
The interior side of the warmer

61C 外底
The exterior side of the warmer

62 单流折柄银铫　唐

Warmer with a spout and a folded handle. Tang dynasty.

63 银则　唐

Ladle. Tang dynasty.

64 银则（3件） 唐
Ladles (3 pieces). Tang dynasty.

65 四曲葵口银勺 唐
Four-lobed and sunflower-rimmed ladle. Tang dynasty.

66 鎏金花草纹银则　唐
Ladle with design of flowers and grass. Tang dynasty.

67 素面兽首衔环耳提梁银罐　唐
Handled pot with a designed lid. Tang dynasty.

68 鎏金鹦鹉纹提梁银罐　唐
Handled pot with design of parrots. Tang dynasty.

69 素面提梁银盖罐　唐
Handled pot with a lid. Tang dynasty.

70 素面平底银罐　唐
Pot with a flat base. Tang dynasty.

71 素面直口银盖罐　唐
Pot with an everted rim. Tang dynasty.

72 素面三足银罐　唐
Three-legged pot . Tang dynasty.

73 素面三足束腰形银罐　唐
Three-legged pot with a concave waist. Tang dynasty.

74 仰莲瓣座银罐　唐
Pot with a lotus-petal-shaped base. Tang dynasty.

75A 莲瓣纹提梁银罐　唐

Handled pot with design of lotus petals. Tang dynasty.

75B 盖内壁墨书

The ink characters on the interior wall of the cover

76 鎏金春秋人物故事纹三足银罐　唐
Three-legged jar with figures in landscape. Tang dynasty.

77 银石榴罐　唐
Pomegranate-shaped pot. Tang dynasty.

78 银石榴罐　唐
Pomegranate-shaped pot. Tang dynasty.

79 鎏金舞马衔杯纹银壶　唐
Flask with design of a dancing horse holding a cup in its mouth. Tang dynasty.

80 “宣徽酒坊”银酒注　唐
Wine pitcher with inscription "*xuan hui jiu fang*". Tang dynasty.

81 “大粒光明砂”银药盒　唐

Cinnabar box with inscription "*da li guang ming sha*" in black ink. Tang dynasty.

82 “次光明砂”银药盒　唐

Cinnabar box with inscription "*ci guang ming sha*" in black ink. Tang dynasty.

83 “红光丹砂”银药盒　唐

Cinnabar box with inscription "*hong guang dan sha*" in black ink. Tang dynasty.

84 “光明碎红砂”银药盒　唐

Cinnabar box with inscription "*guang ming sui hong sha*" in black ink. Tang dynasty.

85 “光明紫砂”银药盒　唐

Cinnabar box with inscription "*guang ming zi sha*" in black ink. Tang dynasty.

86 "上上乳"银药盒　唐
Box with inscription "*shang shang ru*" in black ink. Tang dynasty.

87 "次上乳"银药盒　唐
Box with inscription "*ci shang ru*" in black ink. Tang dynasty.

88A “次乳”银药盒　唐

Box with inscription "*ci ru*" in black ink. Tang dynasty.

88B

89 素面金盒　唐

Box. Tang dynasty.

90 鎏金宝相花纹银盒　唐

Box with design of lotus medallions. Tang dynasty.

91A 鎏金石榴花结纹银盒　唐
Box with design of pomegranate-flower-knots. Tang dynasty.

91B 盒盖外壁
The exterior side of the cover

91C 盒底外壁
The exterior side of the box.

92A 鎏金飞狮纹银盒　唐
Box with design of a flying lion. Tang dynasty.

92B 盒底外壁
The exterior side of the box.

92C 盒底外壁
The exterior side of the box.

93A 鎏金宝相串枝花纹银盒　唐
Box with design of floral strings. Tang dynasty.

93B 盒盖外壁
The exterior side of the cover.

94 鎏金线刻凤鸟纹银盒　唐
Box with design of phoenixes. Tang dynasty.

95 鎏金刻花小银盒　唐
Box with design of engraved flowers. Tang dynasty.

96 鎏金鸳鸯纹小银盒　唐
Box with design of a mandarin duck. Tang dynasty.

97A 鎏金仙鹤翼鹿纹银盒　唐
Box with design of cranes and a winged deer. Tang dynasty.

97B 盒盖外壁及盒底外壁
The exterior sides of the cover and the base.

98A 鎏金翼鹿凤鸟纹银盒 唐
Box with design of a winged deer and a phoenix. Tang dynasty.

98B 盒盖外壁及盒底外壁
The exterior sides of the cover and the base.

99A 鎏金双鸾纹银盒　唐
Box with design of two phoenix-looking birds. Tang dynasty.

99B 盒盖外壁及盒底外壁
The exterior sides of the cover and the base.

100 素面银盒　唐
Box. Tang dynasty.

101 鎏金串枝花纹银盒　唐
Box with design of floral strings. Tang dynasty.

102A 鎏金犀牛石榴花纹银盒　唐
Box with design of a rhino and pomegranate flowers. Tang dynasty.

102B 盒盖外壁及盒底外壁
The exterior sides of the cover and the base.

103 素面银盒　唐
Box. Tang dynasty.

104 鎏金花鸟纹双层银盒　唐
Two-layered box with design of flowers and birds. Tang dynasty.

105 鎏金鹦鹉纹云头形银粉盒　唐
Cloud-head-shaped powder box with design of parrots. Tang dynasty.

106 鎏金鹦鹉卷草纹云头形银粉盒（2件） 唐
Cloud-head-shaped powder box with design of parrots and vine scrolls (2 pieces). Tang dynasty.

107 鎏金蝴蝶纹海棠形银盒 唐
Chinese-flowering-crabapple-shaped box with design of butterflies. Tang dynasty.

108 金襟钩　春秋
Robe hook. Spring and Autumn period.

110 金耳坠（1对）　西周
Earrings (a pair). Western Zhou dynasty.

109 盘羊形银扣饰　战国
Coiled-goat-shaped buckle.
Warring States period.

111 鎏金飞鸟纹银簪　唐
Hairpin with design of flying birds. Tang dynasty.

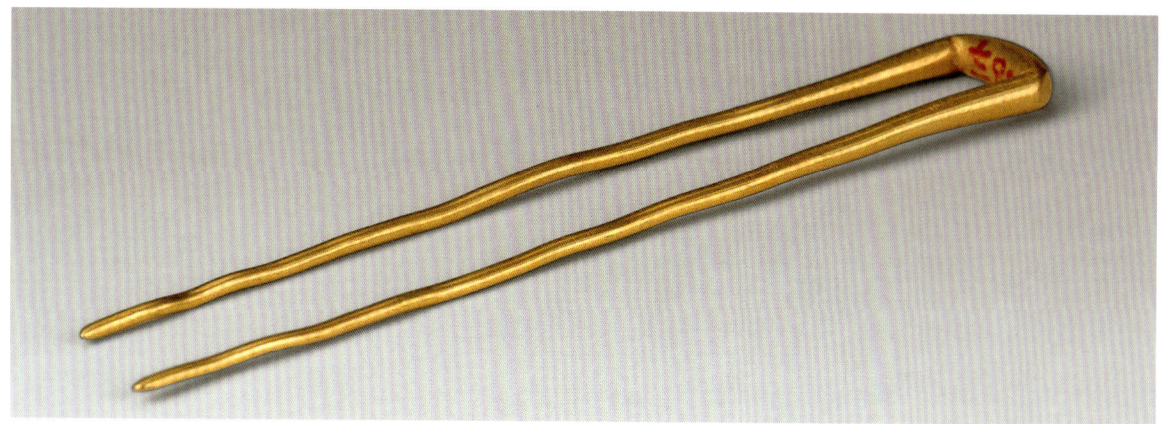

112 素面金钗 唐
Hairpin. Tang dynasty.

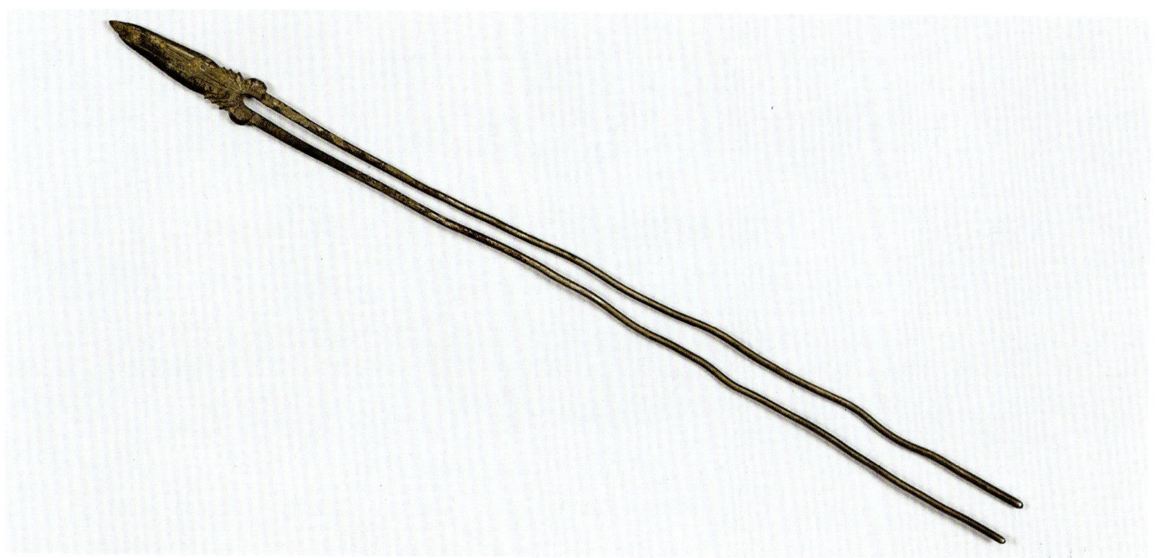

113 花苞头银钗 唐
Hairpin with a flower-bud-shaped final. Tang dynasty.

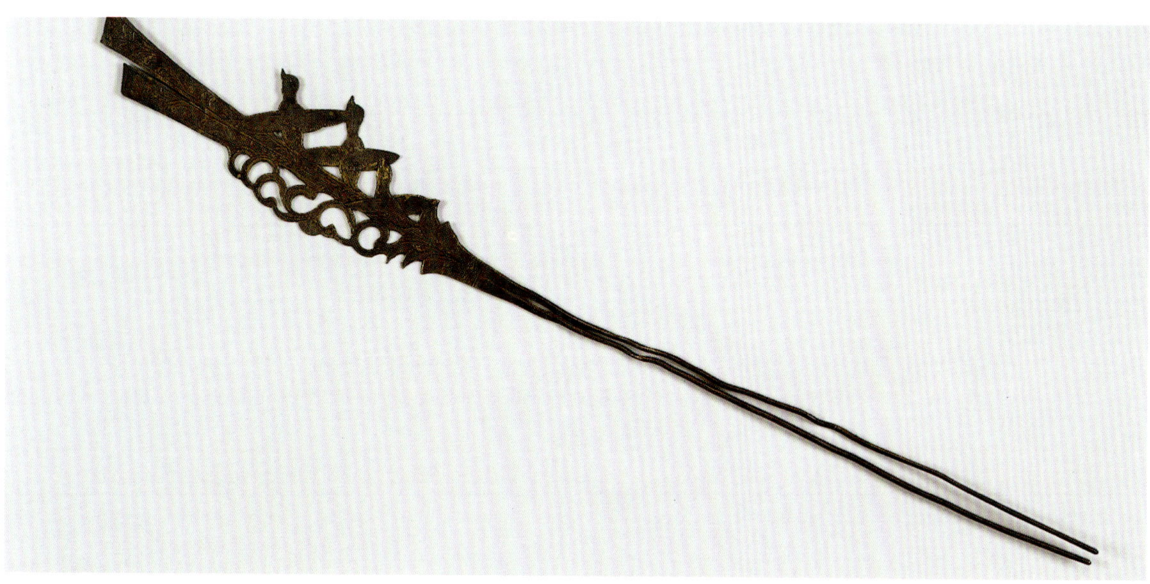

114 鎏金鸿雁纹银钗 唐
Hairpin with design of wild geese. Tang dynasty.

115 鎏金蝴蝶纹银钗　唐

Hairpin with openwork design of butterflies. Tang dynasty.

116 鎏金菊花纹银钗（2件）　唐

Hairpins with openwork design of chrysanthemums (2 pieces). Tang dynasty.

117 鎏金摩羯莲叶纹银钗（2件） 唐
Hairpins with openwork design of Makara and lotus leaves (2 pieces). Tang dynasty.

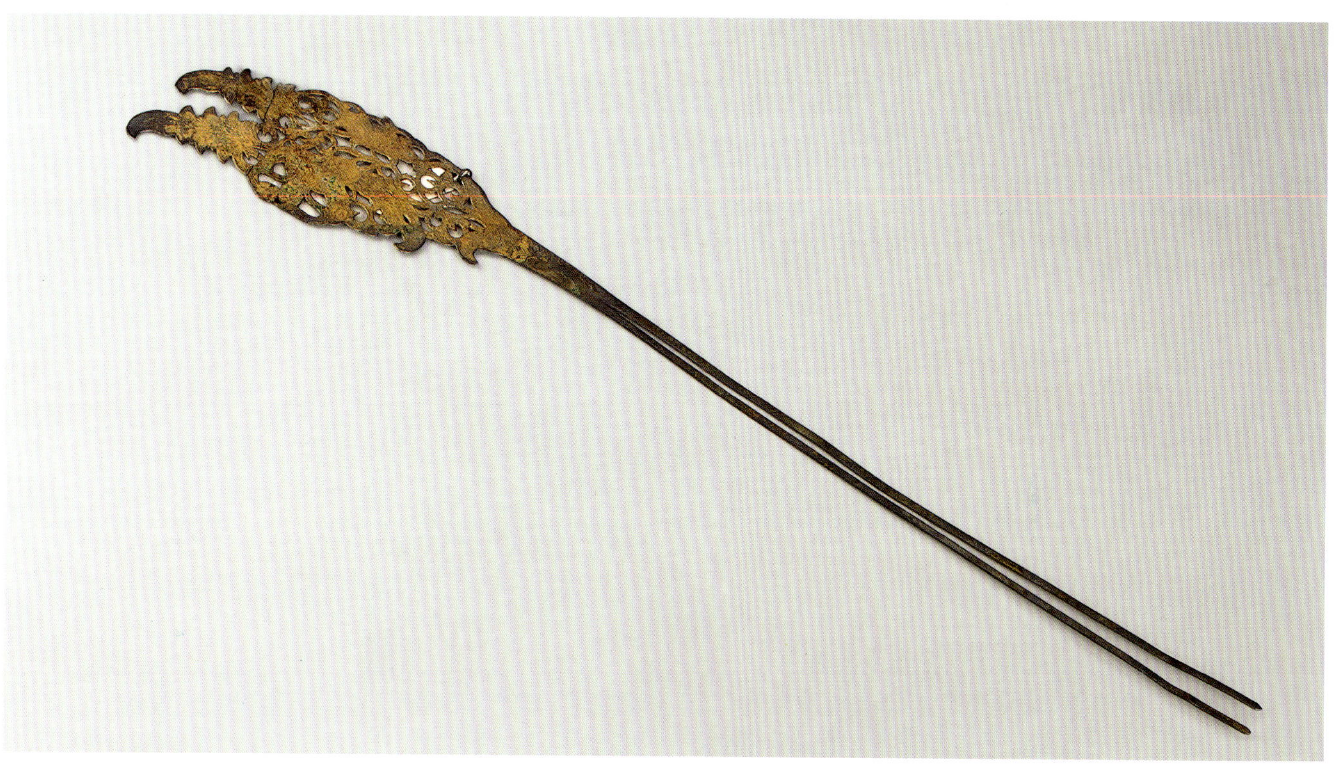

118 鎏金伽陵频嘉纹银钗 唐
Hairpin with openwork design of Kalavinkas. Tang dynasty.

119 鎏金银蝴蝶形头饰　唐
Hairpin in the shape of a butterfly. Tang dynasty.

120 金筐宝钿鸿雁衔枝纹金梳背　唐
Comb-back with filigree design of wild geese holding floral sprays in their mouths. Tang dynasty.

121 金筐宝钿卷草纹金梳背　唐
Comb-back with floral design. Tang dynasty.

122 金臂钏　唐
Armlet. Tang dynasty.

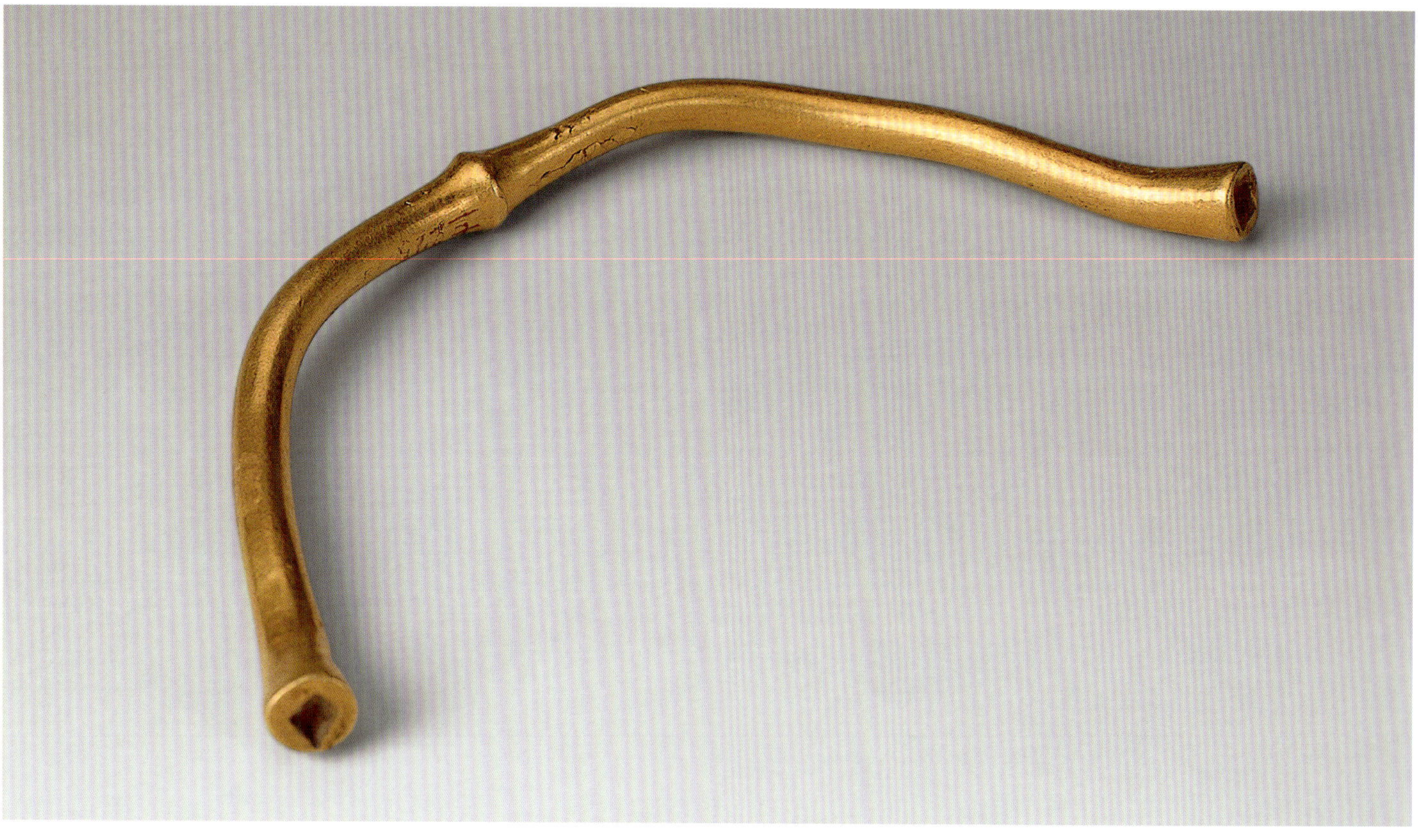

123 竹节形金手镯　唐
Bamboo-joint-shaped bracelet. Tang dynasty.

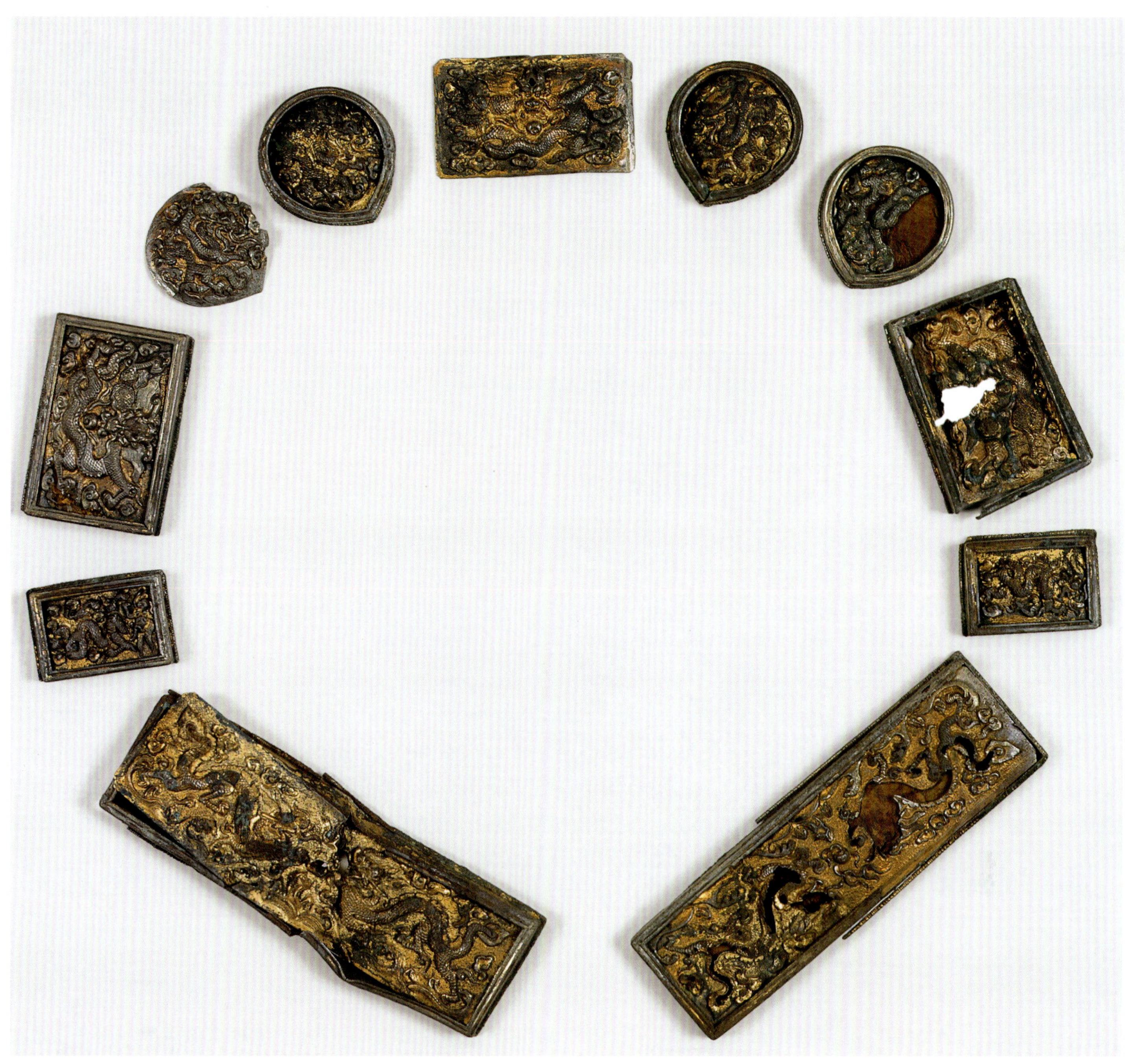

124 鎏金龙纹银带銙　明

Belt plaques with design of dragons. Ming dynasty.

125A 鎏金铜佛像　东魏
Statue of Buddha. Eastern Wei dynasty.

125B 背面
The back side of the statue.

126 银力士像　唐
Statue of Vajrapani. Tang dynasty.

127 银力士像　唐
Statue of Vajrapani. Tang dynasty.

128 银力士像　唐
Statue of Vajrapani. Tang dynasty.

129 银力士像 唐
Statue of Vajrapani. Tang dynasty.

130 银力士像 唐
Statue of Vajrapani. Tang dynasty.

131 鎏金孔雀纹盝顶银宝函　唐
Cube-shaped casket with design of peacocks. Tang dynasty.

132A 鎏金兔纹盝顶银宝函　辽
Cube-shaped casket with design of a rabbit.
Liao dynasty.

132B 盖顶外壁
The exterior side of the cover.

132C 内壁錾文
Inscriptions on the interior bottom of the casket.

132D 正面外壁
The front exterior side.

133 银棺、银宝函　宋

Coffin-shaped reliquary and cube-shaped casket. Song dynasty.

134 金狗　春秋
Dog. Spring and Autumn period.

135 金啄木鸟　春秋
Woodpecker. Spring and Autumn period.

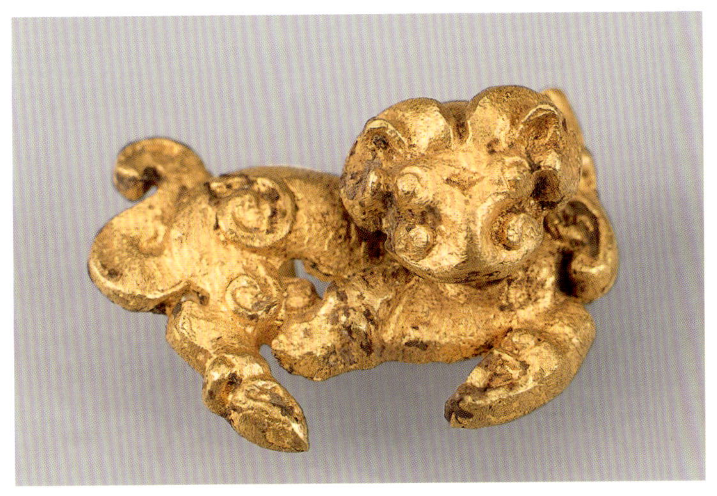

136 金羊虎饰　春秋
Goat-and-tiger-shaped ornament. Spring and Autumn period.

137 金兽形饰　春秋
Beast-shaped ornament. Spring and Autumn period.

138 双鹿纹金牌饰　汉

Plaque with design of two deer. Han dynasty.

139 双驼纹金牌饰　汉

Plaque with design of two camels. Han dynasty.

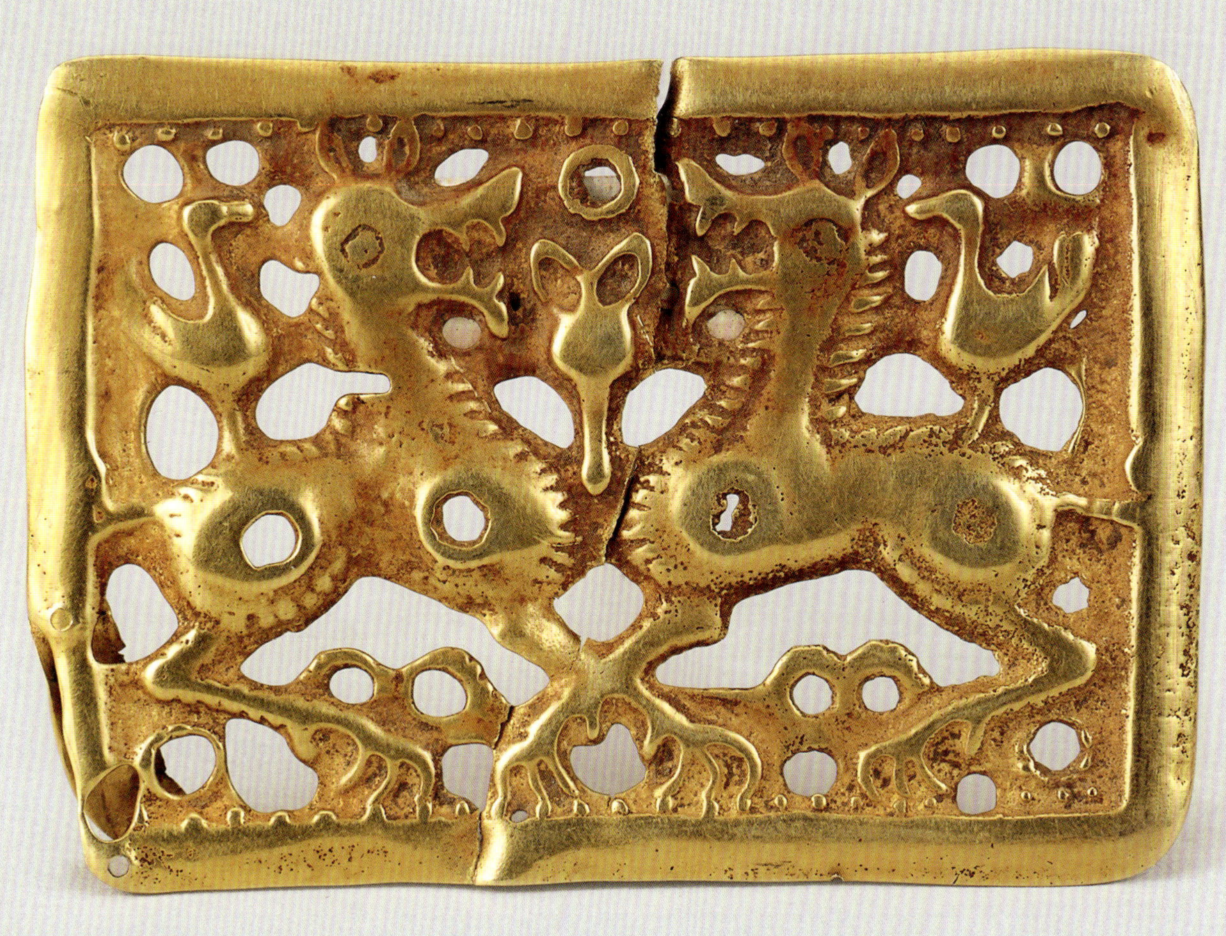

140 双鹿纹金牌饰　汉
Plaque with design of two deer. Han dynasty.

141 银虎　战国～汉
Tiger. Warring states period～Han dynasty.

142 银卧鹿　战国～汉
Crouching deer. Warring states period～Han dynasty.

143A 金鹿形怪兽　战国～汉
Deer-shaped monster. Warring states period～Han dynasty.

143B 尾部
The rear part of the monster.

144 金马形饰件(2件)　汉
Horse-shaped ornaments (2 pieces). Han dynasty.

145 金龙(4条)　唐
Dragons (4 pieces). Tang dynasty.

146 鎏金铁芯铜龙　唐
Dragon. Tang dynasty.

147 鎏金刻花铜羊　唐
Goat with engraved design. Tang dynasty.

148 鎏金银铜竹节熏炉　西汉
Bamboo-joint-shaped censer. Western Han dynasty.

149 鎏金铜虎形镇(2 对)　汉
Paper weights in tiger shape (2 pairs). Han dynasty.

150 鎏金铜铺首(1 对)　汉
Door-knockers (a pair). Han dynasty.

151 鎏金铜铺首　唐
Door-knocker. Tang dynasty.

152 桃形忍冬纹镂空五足银熏炉　唐
Five-legged incense burner with openwork design of peach-shaped honeysuckle scrolls. Tang dynasty.

153A 镂空飞鸟葡萄纹银香囊　唐
Perfumer with openwork design of flying birds and grapes. Tang dynasty.

153B 内部结构
The interior side of the perfumer.

154 鎏金莲花形银灯头　唐
Lotus-flower-shaped lamp top. Tang dynasty.

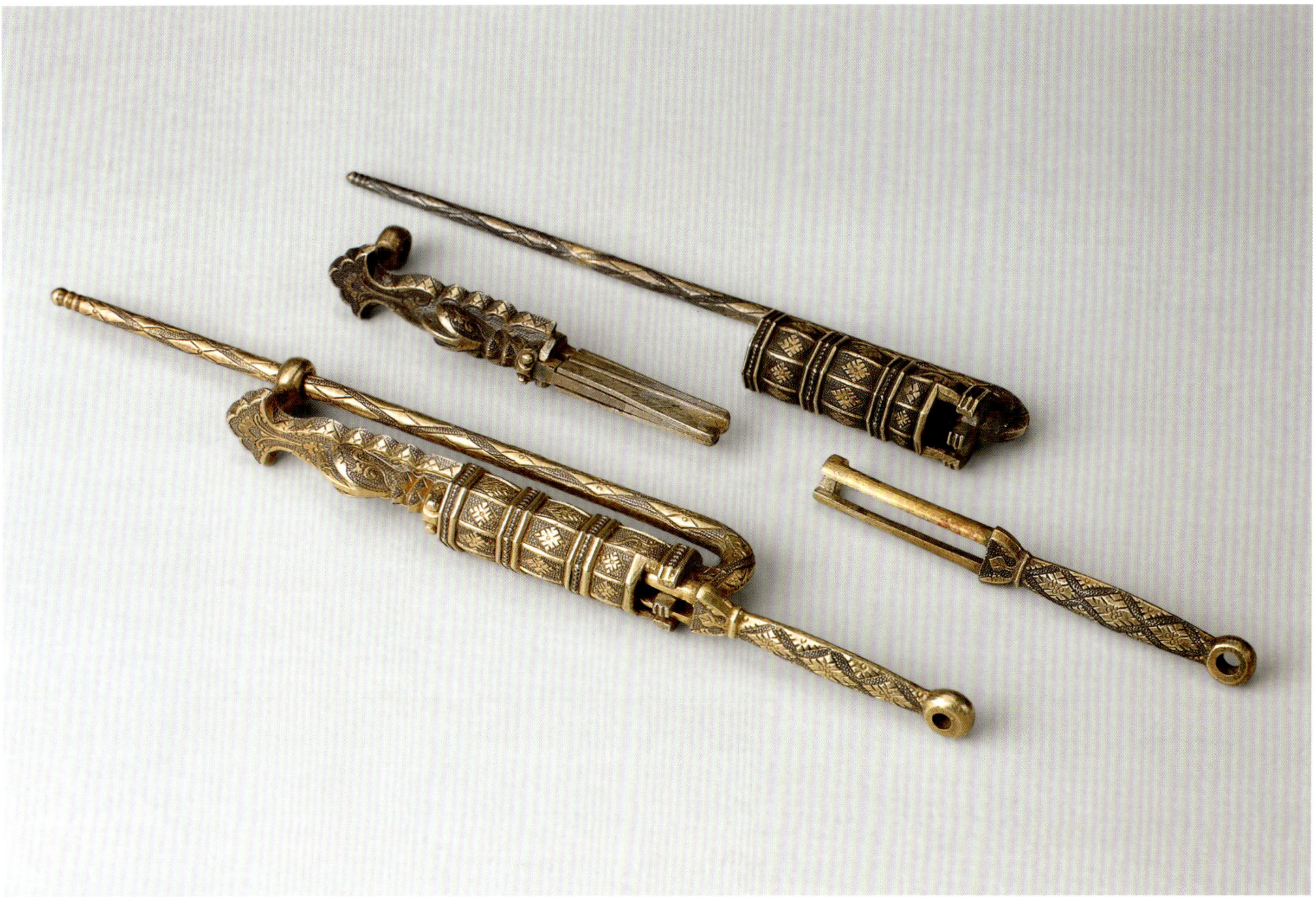

155 鎏金菱纹银锁(2 件)　唐
Padlocks with design of rhombuses (2 pairs). Tang dynasty.

156 鎏金鸿雁纹银渣斗　唐
Spittoon with design of wild geese. Tang dynasty.

157 四鸾衔绶纹金银平脱铜镜　唐
Mirror with inlaid gold and silver design of four phoenixes holding ribbons in their mouths. Tang dynasty.

图版说明

Explanation of Plates

1 **错金银匜**

西汉(公元前206年～公元9年)。1957年陕西省宝鸡市卧龙寺刘家沟出土。高9.9厘米，长径27.4厘米，短径24厘米，重1760克。中国古代，匜和盘相互配合，是一组盥洗器，但也有用以注酒者，《礼记·内则》郑玄注："匜，酒浆器"。汉代银器发现较少，银匜更属少见。此银匜造型与1952年陕西省西安市青门村西汉墓出土的窦氏银匜(现藏中国历史博物馆)类似。

***Yi*, a pouring vessel**

Western Han dynasty (220 B.C.～A.D. 9). Excavated at Liujiagou village, Wolongsi, Baoji city in 1957. Silver with gold inlays. Height: 9.9 cm, long diameter: 27.4 cm, short diameter: 24 cm, weight :1760 g.

2 **鎏金鸿雁衔绶纹银匜**

唐(公元618～907年)。1970年10月陕西省西安市南郊何家村基建工地唐代窖藏出土。通高9.4厘米，口径20.4厘米，足径11.9厘米，流长6.2厘米，重865克。匜内底墨书"廿一两"3字。鸿与雁本为两种飞禽，大曰鸿，小曰雁。由于鸿雁能高飞远翔，古人多以其比喻胸怀大志、有所作为的君子。

***Yi*, a pouring vessel**

Tang dynasty (618～907). Excavated at Hejiacun building site, southern suburbs of Xi'an city in 1970. Silver with gilding. Total height: 9.4cm, diameter of mouth: 20.4 cm, diameter of foot: 11.9 cm, length of spout: 6.2 cm, weight: 865 g.

3 **鎏金鸳鸯鸿雁纹银匜**

唐(公元618～907年)。1970年10月陕西省西安市南郊何家村基建工地唐代窖藏出土。通高9.2厘米，口径19.9厘米，足径11.9厘米，流长6.7厘米，重806克。匜内底墨书"廿一两"3字。

***Yi*, a pouring vessel**

Tang dynasty (618～907). Excavated at Hejiacun building site, southern suburbs of Xi'an city

in 1970. Silver with gilding. Total height: 9.2 cm, diameter of mouth: 19.9 cm, diameter of foot: 11.9 cm, Length of spout: 6.7 cm, weight: 806 g.

4 **素面大银盆**

唐(公元618～907年)。1970年10月陕西省西安市南郊何家村基建工地唐代窖藏出土。高6.5厘米，口径29.4厘米，重1236克。为洗漱用具，可能是与银匜配套使用的。

Basin

Tang dynasty (618～907). Excavated at Hejiacun building site, southern suburbs of Xi'an city in 1970. Silver. Height: 6.5cm, diameter of mouth: 29.4 cm, weight: 1236 g.

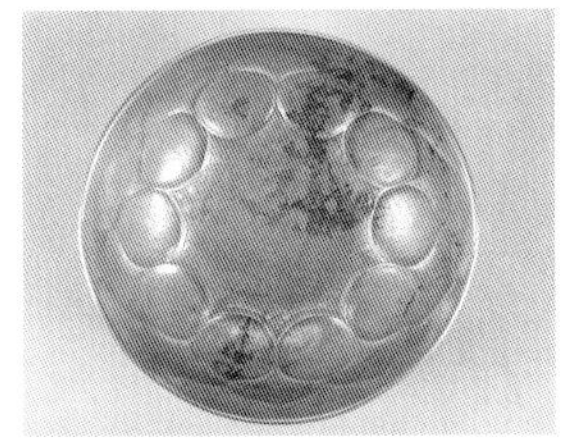

5A-C **鸳鸯莲瓣纹金碗**

唐(公元618～907年)。1970年10月陕西省西安市南郊何家村基建工地唐代窖藏出土。高5.6厘米，口径13.5厘米，足径6.8厘米，重392克。碗内底墨书“九两半”3字。碗的外腹部十分规整地錾刻出上下两层仰莲瓣，每层十瓣，上层每瓣内分别设计一种动物作主题纹饰，有狐狸、兔子、鹿、鸳鸯、鸿雁等，个个栩栩如生，仿佛呼之即出。这种充满生机的流动美，使人强烈地感受到生命跳跃的激情。下层莲瓣内则錾刻相同的忍冬花草，以一种相对的宁静美，来象征万物常存的自然界的永恒。细密的鱼子纹作底衬，则象征多子多福、兴旺发达。金碗的装饰，将生机勃勃、健康向上的时代精神，民族的审美情趣和心理追求，巧妙地融入其中，构思奇特精巧，寓意凝练深远，是金银器满地装的杰作。唐代，皇室贵族饮食讲究使用金质器皿，认为可以辟邪、祛毒，同时，它又是身份等级的一种标志。这件金碗，制作精美绝伦，应该是皇室用物。金碗的制作采用捶揲、錾刻、焊接等多种手法，圆足与碗底焊接处，虽经历一千多年，仍无开裂、脱落，焊缝细密、牢固。金碗内侧墨书的“九两半”仍清晰可辨，这种标重墨书题记，在何家村窖藏的许多金银器上都有，它是唐代宫廷金银器管理留下的遗迹，同时也说明这些器物并未使用过。

Bowl with design of mandarin ducks and lotus petals

Tang dynasty (618～907). Excavated at Hejiacun building site, southern suburbs of Xi'an city in 1970. Gold. Height: 5.6 cm, diameter of mouth: 13.5 cm, diameter of foot: 6.8 cm, weight: 392 g.

6 **鸳鸯莲瓣纹金碗**

唐(公元618～907年)。1970年10月陕西省西安市南郊何家村基建工地唐代窖藏出土。高5.6厘米，口径13.5厘米，足径6.8厘米，重392克。碗内底墨书“九两三”3字。

Bowl with design of mandarin ducks and lotus petals

Tang dynasty (618～907). Excavated at Hejiacun building site, southern suburbs of Xi'an city in 1970. Gold. Height: 5.6 cm, diameter of mouth: 13.5 cm, diameter of foot: 6.8 cm, weight: 392 g.

7 **赤金盆**

唐(公元618～907年)。1970年10月陕西省西安市南郊何家村基建工地唐代窖藏出土。高6.5厘米，口径28.9厘米，重2075克。金盆系锤打成型，器体厚重，盆口略外侈，器壁光滑规整，内底心和外底心经过机械加工，留有螺旋纹痕迹。唐代，金盆是皇宫中使用的洗面用具，皇宫中举行洗儿会，为皇子洗身也用金盆，因此，亦称作洗儿盆或浴盆。

Basin

Tang dynasty (618～907). Excavated at Hejiacun building site, southern suburbs of Xi'an city

in 1970. Pure gold. Height: 6.5 cm, diameter of mouth: 28.9 cm, weight: 2075 g.

8A-C 鎏金海兽水波纹银碗

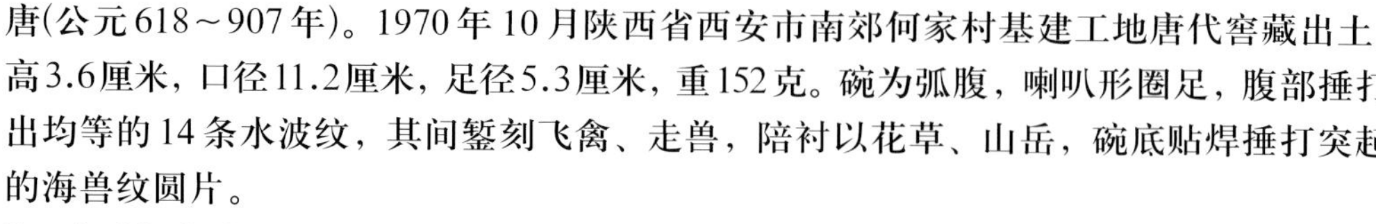

唐(公元618～907年)。1970年10月陕西省西安市南郊何家村基建工地唐代窖藏出土。高3.6厘米，口径11.2厘米，足径5.3厘米，重152克。碗为弧腹，喇叭形圈足，腹部捶打出均等的14条水波纹，其间錾刻飞禽、走兽，陪衬以花草、山岳，碗底贴焊捶打突起的海兽纹圆片。

Bowl with design of sea animals and waves

Tang dynasty (618～907). Excavated at Hejiacun building site, southern suburbs of Xi'an city in 1970. Silver with gilding.Height: 3.6 cm, diameter of mouth: 11.2 cm, diameter of foot: 5.3 cm, weight: 152 g.

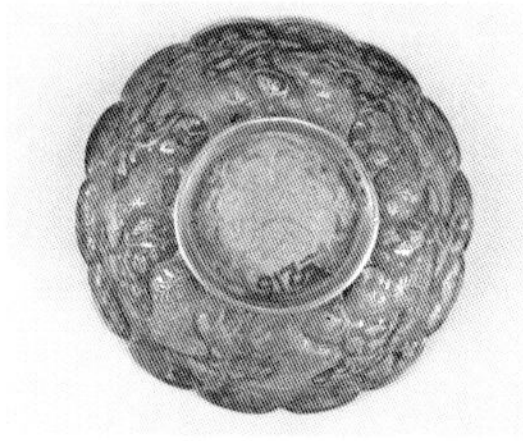

9A-B 鎏金双狮衔枝纹银碗

唐(公元618～907年)。1970年10月陕西省西安市南郊何家村基建工地唐代窖藏出土。高3.7厘米，口径12.6厘米，重201克。碗为侈口、圆底，捶揲成型。碗的腹部均匀地捶打出十朵火焰纹。碗的内底焊接一圆形银片，银片边沿是由索纹、弦纹构成的一周圆圈，里面是双狮衔枝纹，纹饰采用捶打手法制成，并全部鎏金。

Bowl with design of two lions holding floral sprays in their mouths

Tang dynasty (618～907). Excavated at Hejiacun building site, southern suburbs of Xi'an city in 1970. Silver with gilding. Height: 3.7 cm, diameter of mouth: 12.6 cm, weight: 201 g.

10A-B 鎏金双鱼纹银碗

唐(公元618～907年)。1970年10月陕西省西安市南郊何家村基建工地唐代窖藏出土。高2.1厘米，口径11.7厘米，重122克。碗为敞口、斜腹。碗内底采用捶揲法制作出突出的鲵、鱼，周围陪衬以水草，水草亦为捶揲制成。纹饰鎏金，尾、鳍等细部使用錾刻和线刻手法加工。碗腹部内外壁均旋切打光，因此，留有密集的平行线状的细纹。

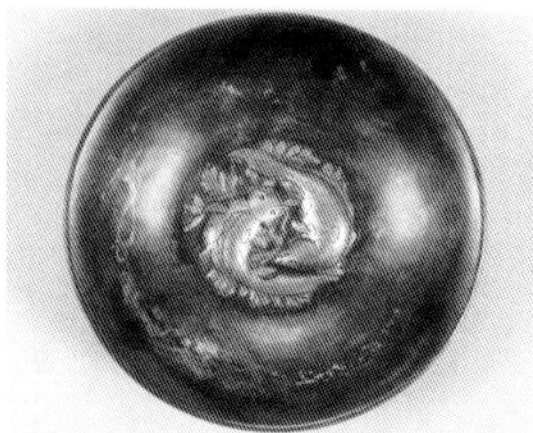

Bowl with design of two fish

Tang dynasty (618～907). Excavated at Hejiacun building site, southern suburbs of Xi'an city in 1970. Silver with gilding. Height: 2.1 cm, diameter of mouth: 11.7 cm, weight: 122 g.

11 鎏金花鸟纹银碗

唐(公元618～907年)。1970年10月陕西省西安市南郊何家村基建工地唐代窖藏出土。高3.3厘米，口径10.3厘米，重136克。碗内壁錾折枝莲并衬以流云，外壁錾忍冬石榴卷草五组，每组中间錾鸳鸯等珍禽，内外底均錾蔷薇式团花一朵。纹饰全部鎏金。

Bowl with design of flowers and birds

Tang dynasty (618～907). Excavated at Hejiacun building site, southern suburbs of Xi'an city

in 1970. Silver with gilding. Height: 3.3 cm, diameter of mouth: 10.3 cm, weight: 136 g.

12 鎏金花鸟纹银碗

唐(公元618～907年)。1970年10月陕西省西安市南郊何家村基建工地唐代窖藏出土。高3厘米，口径10厘米，重130克。

Bowl with design of flowers and birds

Tang dynasty (618～907). Excavated at Hejiacun building site, southern suburbs of Xi'an city in 1970. Silver with gilding. Height: 3 cm, diameter of mouth: 10 cm, weight: 130 g.

13A-B 鎏金蔓草龙凤纹银碗

唐(公元618～907年)。1970年10月陕西省西安市南郊何家村基建工地唐代窖藏出土。高4.9厘米，口径12.8厘米，足径7厘米，重158克。碗内底錾刻一只展翅凤凰，足下为葡萄忍冬卷草纹，外底圈足内錾刻一团身飞龙，衬以流云，纹饰细腻流畅，雕刻精湛细密，是满地装的典范。如此龙凤图案布局，在唐代金银器中仅见。中国古代，龙和凤是神灵动物，封建社会，统治阶级常常用龙凤来象征皇权，标榜美德，这件银碗是实用器，有明显的使用痕迹，当是皇宫内皇帝、皇后使用的器物。

Bowl with design of dragon, phoenix and vine scrolls

Tang dynasty (618～907). Excavated at Hejiacun building site, southern suburbs of Xi'an city in 1970. Silver with gilding. Height: 4.9 cm, diameter of mouth: 12.8 cm, diameter of foot: 7 cm, weight: 158 g.

14 素面金碗

唐(公元618～907年)。1970年10月陕西省西安市南郊何家村基建工地唐代窖藏出土。高6.5厘米，口径15.1厘米，足径7.7厘米，重550克。

Bowl

Tang dynasty (618～907). Excavated at Hejiacun building site, southern suburbs of Xi'an city in 1970. Gold. Height 6.5 cm, diameter of mouth: 15.1 cm, diameter of foot: 7.7 cm, weight: 550 g.

15 素面卵形银碗

唐(公元618～907年)。1970年10月陕西省西安市南郊何家村基建工地唐代窖藏出土。高4厘米，口径10.1～11.6厘米，重215克。

Bowl

Tang dynasty (618～907). Excavated at Hejiacum building site, suburbs of Xi'an city in 1970. Silver. Diameter of mouth: 10.1～11.6 cm, weight: 215 g.

16 素面银碗

唐(公元618～907年)。1970年10月陕西省西安市南郊何家村基建工地唐代窖藏出土。高4.3厘米，口径12.3厘米，足径5.4厘米，重152克。

Bowl

Tang dynasty (618～907). Excavated at Hejiacun building site, southern suburbs of Xi'an city in 1970. Silver. Total height: 4.3cm, diameter of mouth: 12.3 cm, diameter of foot: 5.4 cm, weight: 152 g.

17 **素面银碗**

唐(公元618～907年)。1970年10月陕西省西安市南郊何家村基建工地唐代窖藏出土。高4.7厘米，口径11.7厘米，足径5.9厘米，重148克。

Bowl

Tang dynasty (618～907). Excavated at Hejiacun building site, southern suburbs of Xi'an city in 1970. Silver. Height: 4.7 cm, diameter of mouth: 11.7 cm, diameter of foot: 5.9 cm, weight: 148 g.

18A-B **素面银碗**

唐(公元618～907年)。1970年10月陕西省西安市南郊何家村基建工地唐代窖藏出土。高7.4厘米，口径18.6厘米，足径10.7厘米，重624克。碗内底墨书“十五两一分”5字。据《唐六典》记载，唐代度量衡有大制、小制两种，官民日常用大制，调钟律、测晷影、合汤药及冠冕之制用小制。据现发表的唐代衡制资料看，1两多在40～42克之间。按此银碗重量及墨书标重题记算，1两为41.32克。

Bowl

Tang dynasty (618～907). Excavated at Hejiacun building site, southern suburbs of Xi'an city in 1970. Silver. Height: 7.4cm, diameter of mouth: 18.6 cm, diameter of foot: 10.7 cm, weight: 624 g.

19 **鎏金折枝花纹银盖碗**

唐(公元618～907年)。1970年10月陕西省西安市南郊何家村基建工地唐代窖藏出土。通高11.9厘米，口径21.8厘米，足径12.2厘米，重1380克。碗盖内面及碗内底分别墨书“二斤一两并底”、“二斤一两并盖”。

Lidded bowl with design of floral sprays

Tang dynasty (618～907). Excavated at Hejiacun building site, southern suburbs of Xi'an city in 1970. Silver with gilding. Total height: 11.9 cm, diameter of mouth: 21.8 cm, diameter of foot: 12.2 cm, weight: 1380 g.

20A-B **鎏金小簇花纹银盖碗**

唐(公元618～907年)。1970年10月陕西省西安市南郊何家村基建工地唐代窖藏出土。通高9.9厘米，口径21.6厘米，足径12厘米，重1220克。盖碗是盛放羹汤的器具，随着饮食文化的发展，上流贵族对饮食器也越来越讲究。此碗在装饰上采用散点式手法，盖顶中心錾刻出一朵六出大团花，周围及腹部散点式地配置了六朵向心式小簇花，纹饰全部鎏金，显得简洁大方，一目了然。碗盖内面及碗内底分别墨书“卅两并底”、“卅两并盖”，盖捉手内沿刻“卅两一分”，底圈足内沿刻“卅两三分”，反映出此盖碗为未使用的器物，皇宫内对带盖类器物的管理是很严的。

Lidded bowl with design of floral clusters

Tang dynasty (618～907). Excavated at Hejiacun building site, southern suburbs of Xi'an city in 1970. Silver with gilding. Total height: 9.9 cm; diameter of mouth: 21.6 cm, diameter of foot: 12 cm; weight: 1220 g .

21 鎏金宝相花纹银盖碗

唐(公元618～907年)。1970年10月陕西省西安市南郊何家村基建工地唐代窖藏出土。高8.4厘米，盖高3.4厘米，盖径21.6厘米，重1421克。碗盖内面及碗底分别墨书“二斤一两并底”、“三斤二两并盖”。

Lidded bowl with design of floral medallions

Tang dynasty (618～907). Excavated at Hejiacun building site, southern suburbs of Xi'an city in 1970. Silver with gilding. Total height: 8.4 cm, diameter of the lid: 21.6 cm, height of the lid: 3.4 cm, weight: 1421 g.

22 鎏金鱼纹银碗

唐(公元618～907年)。1983年10月陕西省西安市东郊二道巷服装公司工地出土。高5.2厘米，口径13.1厘米，足径6.9厘米，重48克。

Bowl with design of fish

Tang dynasty (618～907). Excavated at Erdaoxiang Costume Company building site, eastern suburbs of Xi'an city in 1983. Silver with gilding. Height: 5.2 cm, diameter of mouth: 13.1 cm, diameter of foot: 6.9 cm, weight: 48 g.

23 鎏金鸿雁纹四曲银碗

唐(公元618～907年)。1958年春陕西省耀县柳林背阴村出土。高7.1厘米，口径18.6厘米，足径11.6厘米，重391克。

Four-lobed bowl with design of wild geese

Tang dynasty (618～907). Excavated at Beiyin village, Liulin, Yaoxian in 1958. Silver with gilding. Height: 7.1 cm, diameter of mouth: 18.6 cm, diameter of foot: 11.6 cm, weight: 391 g.

24A-B “宣徽酒坊”银碗

唐(公元618～907年)。1958年春陕西省耀县柳林背阴村出土。高5.1厘米，口径14.7厘米，足径7.7厘米，重312克。碗底圈足内錾有“宣徽酒坊／宇字号”2行7字。唐代宣徽院“置宣徽南北院使以宦者任之，总领内诸司及三班内侍之籍，郊祀、朝会、宴飨、供帐之事”。宣徽酒坊是宣徽院所属的酒坊，其所用银器是按《千字文》的“天地玄黄，宇宙洪荒”等文字顺序编排号码的，由碗底錾文可知，这件银碗的编号是“宇”字。

Bowl with inscription of "*xuan hui jiu fang*"

Tang dynasty (618～907). Excavated at Beiyin village, Liulin, Yaoxian in 1958. Silver. Height: 5.1 cm, diameter of mouth: 14.7 cm, diameter of foot: 7.7 cm, weight: 312 g.

25 鎏金蔓草花鸟纹高足银杯

唐(公元618～907年)。1982年陕西省西安市东郊纬十街电车二场工地出土。高6.1厘米，口径7.6厘米，足径4.1厘米，重95克。银杯为侈口，外壁下部饰一周凸棱，腹壁捶打出十个莲瓣，每个莲瓣内均饰花鸟纹，圈足作覆莲瓣形，饰以忍冬纹。纹饰錾刻，全部鎏金。据齐东方先生研究，这种造型的高足杯可能是受拜占廷金银器物影响而制作的。

High-footed cup with design of flowers, birds and vine scrolls

Tang dynasty (618～907). Excavated at the building site of Weishi Street Trolley Lot, eastern suburbs of Xi'an in 1982. Silver with gilding. Height: 6.1 cm, diameter of mouth: 7.6 cm, diameter of foot: 4.1 cm, weight: 95 g.

26 **狩猎纹高足银杯**

唐(公元618～907年)。1970年10月陕西省西安市南郊何家村基建工地唐代窖藏出土。高7.2厘米，口径6厘米，重100克。唐代统治者对武艺、军备极为重视，皇帝及一般贵族都非常喜爱狩猎，太宗李世民将狩猎放在与国家统一、国泰民安同等重要的位置，提出了他的著名的人生三乐之说，巢王李元吉更是痴迷狩猎："我宁三日不食，不可一日不猎"。因此，狩猎活动成为器物装饰流行的题材。银杯底足刻有"马舍"二字。

High-footed cup with design of hunting scene

Tang dynasty (618～907). Excavated at Hejiacun building site, southern suburbs of Xi'an city in 1970. Silver. Height: 7.2 cm, diameter of mouth: 6 cm, diameter of foot: 4 cm, weight 100 g.

27 **金筐宝钿团花纹金杯**

唐(公元618～907年)。高6厘米，口径6.9厘米，足径3.16厘米，重230克。1970年10月陕西省西安市南郊何家村基建工地唐代窖藏出土。金杯捶揲成型后，进行旋切打磨，因此腹身处留有密集的等距离的平行线。然后将厚0.5毫米、宽1毫米的金条编成花纹焊接在腹部，花纹内原镶嵌有宝石，花纹外侧焊接一周直径1毫米的小金珠。鋬手是用宽5～7毫米、厚1.5毫米的金条折成的，鋬手下垫十字花形金片，最后用铆钉固定在杯腹上。

Cup with filigree design of stylized flower medallions

Tang dynasty (618～907). Excavated at Hejiacun building site, southern suburbs of Xi'an city in 1970. Gold. Height: 6 cm, diameter of mouth: 6.9 cm, diameter of foot: 3.16 cm, weight: 230 g.

28A-B **鎏金仕女狩猎纹八瓣银杯**

唐(公元618～907年)。1970年10月陕西省西安市南郊何家村基建工地唐代窖藏出土。高5.1厘米，口径9.1厘米，足径3.8厘米，重209克。银杯的花纹装饰，分布在外壁的八朵花瓣内。八朵花瓣又以柳叶条带作界栏，形成八幅既独立又相互关联的画面。四幅男子狩猎图中，男子身着袍衫，跃马奔驰在丛林当中，或搭弓回射飞禽，或持刀追杀野兔，或抛投绳索，套捕獐子，或紧追仓皇逃窜的花鹿。四幅仕女图中，妇女或乐舞，或戏婴，或梳妆，或游玩。小小的八幅画，就把唐代男子与妇女生活中重要的一幕情景勾勒出来，动与静的节律，紧张与悠闲的气氛都处理得恰到好处，很有艺术感染力。银杯的内底处，以水波纹为底衬，中间錾刻出一个摩羯头和三尾小鱼，凹陷的八只莲瓣内相间地錾刻出花草。这样，当杯中盛放酒或水以后，仿佛在微波荡漾的池中，鱼儿游动，水草漂浮，给平凡的饮食生活增添了几许观赏乐趣。

Octagonal-shaped cup with design of ladies and hunting scene

Tang dynasty (618～907). Excavated at Hejiacun building site, southern suburbs of Xi'an city in 1970. Silver with gilding. Height: 5.1 cm, diameter of mouth: 9.1 cm, diameter of foot: 3.8 cm, weight: 209 g.

29 **伎乐纹八棱金杯**

唐(公元618～907年)。1970年10月陕西省西安市南郊何家村基建工地唐代窖藏出土。高6.1厘米，口径6厘米，重380克。杯为侈口、圜底、喇叭形圈足。环柄平鋬上饰两个相连的深目高鼻、长髯的胡人头像，柄外侧有兽头，内侧与杯身焊接。器身八棱，以联珠为界栏，每面饰胡人乐伎一人，分别执拍板、小铙、洞箫、曲颈琵琶，或抱壶、执杯。据学者研究，这件银杯是从粟特地区传来的舶来品。

Octagonal-shaped cup with design of musicians

Tang dynasty (618～907). Excavated at Hejiacun building site, southern suburbs of Xi'an city in 1970. Gold. Height: 6.1 cm, diameter of mouth: 6 cm, weight: 380 g.

30A-C **鎏金胡人伎乐纹八棱银杯**

唐(公元618～907年)。1970年10月陕西省西安市南郊何家村基建工地唐代窖藏出土。高6.7厘米，口径6.9～7.4厘米，足径4.4厘米，重285克。八棱形杯身每面有浮雕式胡人乐伎一名，深目高鼻，头戴卷檐尖帽或瓦楞帽，分别执拍板、小铙、洞箫、曲颈琵琶等乐器，另有抱壶、执杯及两名空手舞蹈者。据学者研究， 此杯为粟特工匠的制品。生活在中亚地区的粟特人，极善经商，其足迹遍及欧亚内陆，不少粟特人移居中国，对中国的手工制造业发生了很大的影响，中国境内发现不少从粟特地区传入的银器，同时也出现了唐代工匠仿粟特器物制造的金银器皿。这件银杯有可能就是生活在中国的粟特工匠制造的，造型上已开始有了一些变化。

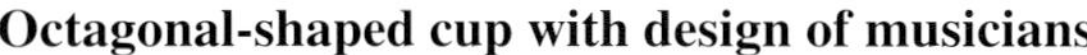

Octagonal-shaped cup with design of musicians

Tang dynasty (618～907). Excavated at Hejiacun building site, southern suburbs of Xi'an city in 1970. Silver with gilding. Height: 6.7 cm, diameter of mouth: 6.9～7.4 cm, diameter of foot: 4.4 cm, weight: 285 g.

31A-B **人物纹八棱金杯**

唐(公元618～907年)。1970年10月陕西省西安市南郊何家村基建工地唐代窖藏出土。高5.6厘米，口径5.7～7.2厘米，足径3.2厘米，重225克。杯体八面以联珠作界栏，每栏内各有浮雕式人物一名，除一人双手合十、袒胸露腹外，其余均穿窄袖翻领胡袍，束带着靴，衣纹、面容等细部均精心錾刻，人物衬以忍冬卷草。环形柄的云头状鋬上錾刻一深目高鼻、长髯下垂的胡人头像。圈足沿饰一周球状联珠。从造型和装饰来看，虽然还有浓重的粟特银器的特点，但中国的特点已很明显，有可能是生活在中国的粟特工匠制作的，也有可能是中国工匠仿粟特银杯制作的。

Octagonal-shaped cup with design of figures

Tang dynasty (618～907). Excavated at Hejiacun building site, southern suburbs of Xi'an city in 1970. Gold.Height: 5.6 cm, diameter of mouth: 5.7～7.2 cm, diameter of foot: 3.2 cm, weight: 225 g.

32 **鎏金蔓草纹八棱银杯**

唐(公元618～907年)。1982年陕西省西安市东郊纬十街电车二场工地出土。高5.9厘米，口径7.2厘米，重121克。

Octagonal-shaped cup with design of vine scrolls

Tang dynasty (618～907). Excavated at the building site of Weishi Street Trolley Lot, eastern suburbs of Xi'an city in 1982. Silver with gilding. Height: 5.9 cm, diameter of mouth: 7.2 cm, weight: 121g.

33 素面单环柄银杯

唐(公元618～907年)。1970年10月陕西省西安市南郊何家村基建工地唐代窖藏出土。高9.7厘米，口径9.1厘米，足径7厘米，重391克。器壁较厚，在腹及底部均留有旋切形成的等距离细线纹，底部的中心点还清晰可见。据齐东方先生研究，这件腹部呈罐形的带把银杯是从中亚传入中国的粟特银器。

Water vessel with single-ringed handle

Tang dynasty (618～907). Excavated at Hejiacun building site, southern suburbs of Xi'an city in 1970. Silver. Height: 9.7 cm, diameter of mouth: 9.1 cm, diameter of foot: 7 cm, weight: 391 g.

34 鎏金蔓草鸳鸯纹银羽觞(2件)

唐(公元618～907年)。1970年10月陕西省西安市南郊何家村基建工地唐代窖藏出土。分别高3.2厘米，长10.6厘米，宽9.5厘米，重145克。羽觞又叫耳杯，是古人饮酒用具。此器采用满地装手法，器内外壁均满饰鱼子纹地，主花纹有折枝、团花、卷草、鸳鸯等，均鎏金，显得华丽、富贵。

Cups with design of mandarin ducks and vine scrolls (2 pieces)

Tang dynasty (618～907). Excavated at Hejiacun building site, southern suburbs of Xi'an city in 1970. Silver with gilding. Height: 3.2 cm, length: 10.6 cm, width: 9.5 cm, weight: 145 g.

35 鎏金摩羯纹银长杯

唐(公元618～907年)。1955年陕西省西安市文管会移交。残高3.3厘米，长径12.4厘米，短径6.7厘米，重54克。底部圈足已残缺，仅留有直径约2厘米的疤痕。杯口呈椭圆形，杯体分四曲，是萨珊银器影响下出现的仿制品。

Cup with design of Makara

Tang dynasty (618～907). Handed in by the Cultural Relics Committee of Xi'an City in 1955. Silver with gilding. Height: 3.3 cm, long diameter: 12.4 cm, short diameter: 6.7 cm, weight: 54 g.

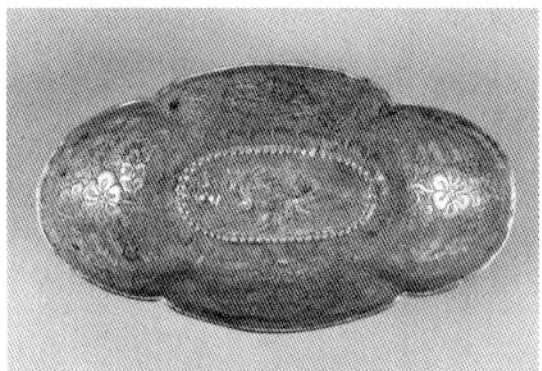

36A-B 摩羯纹金长杯

唐(公元618～907年)。1970年陕西省西安市太乙路出土。高3.5厘米，口长13.1厘米，宽7.5厘米，重174克。杯内底中心捶揲出凸起的摩羯戏宝珠图案，底纹是錾刻细密的水波纹。在印度古神话中，摩羯是一种长鼻利齿、鱼身鱼尾的神异动物，被尊奉为河水之精、生命之本。从公元前3世纪中叶开始，摩羯就出现在古代印度的雕塑、绘画中，东晋时传入中国，到了唐代，摩羯在金银器的装饰中较为常见，但形象已变得复杂、神异，具有明显的中国特点。

Cup with design of Makara

Tang dynasty (618～907). Excavated at Taiyi Road, Xi'an city in 1970. Gold. Height: 3.5 cm, length of mouth: 13.1 cm,width: 7.5 cm, weight: 174 g.

37 五曲高足银杯

唐(公元618～907年)。1958年春陕西省耀县柳林背阴村出土。高8.6厘米，口径9.8厘米，足高3.7厘米，重104克。银杯为花瓣形杯身，喇叭形高圈足，是晚唐流行的样式。

Five-lobed and high-footed cup

Tang dynasty (618～907). Excavated at Beiyin village, Liulin, Yaoxian in 1958. Silver. Height: 8.6 cm, diameter of mouth: 9.8 cm, height of foot: 3.7 cm, weight: 104 g.

38 **金杯坯**

唐(公元618～907年)。1965年春陕西省西安市南郊白庙村出土。高6.2厘米，口径7.1厘米，足径3.5厘米，重170克。此杯从器形看，是高足杯的形状，似乎是在冶铸过程中没有掌握好，造成制作上的失败。

Semi-finished cup

Tang dynasty (618～907). Excavated at Baimiao village, southern suburbs of Xi'an city in 1965. Gold. Height: 6.2 cm, diameter of mouth: 7.1 cm, diameter of foot: 3.5 cm, weight:170 g.

39 **金杯坯**

唐(公元618～907年)。1965年春陕西省西安市南郊白庙村出土。高8.3厘米，口径7.7厘米，重387克。为单把杯造型，把及腹部花纹均用铆钉固定，但铆钉又未穿透腹壁。

Semi-finished cup

Tang dynasty (618～907). Excavated at Baimiao village, southern suburbs of Xi'an city in 1965. Gold. Height: 8.3 cm, diameter of mouth: 7.7 cm, weight: 387 g.

40 **鎏金龟纹桃形银盘**

唐(公元618～907年)。1970年10月陕西省西安市南郊何家村基建工地唐代窖藏出土。高1.2厘米，直径12.3～12.8厘米，重146克。盘心捶打出一只突起的乌龟，细部錾刻，通体鎏金，头颈似缩，两只小圆眼警惕地盯着四方，四爪张开，短尾轻摆，如在缓慢移动，极富写实性。中国古代有用桃驱鬼辟邪的习俗，唐代，道教流行，道家讲究修炼身心、追求长生不老的思想，对王公贵族和文人墨客产生了深刻的影响，桃因甘甜可口且能消灾辟邪，受到人们的普遍喜爱，也成为道家重要的供品。龟坚忍长寿，古人认为它能卜知吉凶、捍难避害。将桃的造型和龟的纹饰巧妙地融为一体，包含着消灾辟邪、长生不老的深刻寓意，是不可多得的唐代艺术珍品。

Cut-peach-shaped dish with design of a turtle

Tang dynasty (618～907). Excavated at Hejiacun building site, southern suburbs of Xi'an city in 1970. Silver with gilding. Height: 1.2 cm, diameter: 12.3～12.8 cm,weight: 146 g.

41 **鎏金双狐纹双桃形银盘**

唐(公元618～907年)。1970年10月陕西省西安市南郊何家村基建工地唐代窖藏出土。高1.5厘米，口径22.5厘米，重322克。狐属哺乳纲食肉目犬科动物，在我国分布很广，很早以前古人就对狐的狡猾、多疑的特点有所认识，形成许多有关狐的成语故事，如狐埋狐揞、狐假虎威。唐代长安城中狐很多，有关狐神、狐妖作祟的传说记载比比皆是。相传狐能修炼成精，化为人形，神通广大，如加触犯，必受其害。“唐初以来，百姓多事狐神，房中祭祀以乞恩，食饮与人同之。”银盘作成桃形并以狐来装饰，具有驱邪辟祟、祈求平安的寓意。

Double-peach-shaped dish with design of two foxes

Tang dynasty (618～907). Excavated at Hejiacun building site, southern suburbs of Xi'an city in 1970. Silver with gilding. Height: 1.5 cm, diameter of mouth: 22.5 cm, weight: 322 g.

42 **鎏金熊纹六曲银盘**

唐(公元618～907年)。1970年10月陕西省西安市南郊何家村基建工地唐代窖藏出土。高1厘米，口径13.4厘米，重140克。熊作仰首咆哮状，形态自然逼真。《诗经》曰：“吉梦维何，维熊维罴。”古人认为梦见熊罴是生男的预兆。

Six-lobed dish with design of a bear

Tang dynasty (618～907). Excavated at Hejiacun building site, southern suburbs of Xi'an city in 1970. Height: 1 cm, diameter of mouth:13.4 cm, weight: 140 g.

43 **鎏金飞廉纹六曲银盘**

唐(公元618～907年)。1970年10月陕西省西安市南郊何家村基建工地唐代窖藏出土。高1.4厘米，口径15.8厘米，重313克。盘中心鼓翼扬尾的动物，原定名为翼牛或异兽，孙机先生考证认为应该是飞廉，飞廉是中国古代神话传说中的兴风之神。在萨珊银盘装饰中，有一种名为塞穆鲁的神兽形象，在粟特银盘装饰中，塞穆鲁被类似的有翼骆驼代替了，唐代工匠又用本民族的飞廉代替了有翼骆驼，而且还突破了粟特银盘单一的圆形平面，将盘口作成唐土流行的六曲花瓣形，反映出唐代工匠对外来文化大胆筛选、借鉴利用的胆略和气魄。

Six-lobed dish with design of a phoenix-looking bird

Tang dynasty (618～907). Excavated at Hejiacun building site, southern suburbs of Xi'an city in 1970. Silver with gilding. Height: 1.4 cm, diameter of mouth: 15.8 cm, weight: 313 g.

44 **鎏金鸾鸟纹六曲银盘**

唐(公元618～907年)。1970年10月陕西省西安市南郊何家村基建工地唐代窖藏出土。高1.5厘米，口径16.3厘米，重220克。银盘为窄平折沿，浅腹，平底，捶打成型，盘心鸾鸟亦捶打成突起状，纹饰鎏金。

Six-lobed dish with design of a phoenix

Tang dynasty (618～907). Excavated at Hejiacun building site, southern suburbs of Xi'an city in 1970. Silver with gilding. Height: 1.5 cm, diameter of mouth: 16.3 cm, weight: 220 g.

45 **鎏金“裴肃进”双凤纹六曲银盘**

唐(公元618～907年)。1962年陕西省西安市北郊坑底寨出土。高3.5厘米，直径54.6厘米，重3250克。盘背面錾刻铭文3行41 字：“浙东道督团练观察处置等使／大中大夫守越州刺史兼御史大夫上柱国赐紫金鱼袋臣裴肃进／点过讫”。由此可知，这件银盘是裴肃向皇帝所行的进奉物。进奉是朝廷官员或地方高级官员向皇帝所行的额外贡献，主要是供皇帝私人使用的，进奉的物品主要有金银、珍宝、钱帛、骏马等，其中金银器占很大的比例。唐德宗时，裴肃为常州刺史，在任期间就贪污敛财，后因进奉升迁为浙东观察使，“天下刺史进奉，自肃始。”这件银盘作为裴肃进奉物的唯一代表，为研究中唐时期社会风气的衰败，提供了珍贵的实物资料。银盘出土于唐大明宫遗址内，当属皇家用物。

Dish with design of two phoenixes

Tang dynasty (618～907). Excavated at Kengdizhai, northern suburbs of Xi'an city in 1962. Silver with gilding. Height: 3.5 cm, diameter: 54.6 cm, weight: 3250 g.

46 **鎏金凤鸟纹葵形大银盘(残)**

唐(公元618～907年)。1956年陕西省西安市东郊韩森寨出土。为迄今所见直径最大的唐代银盘。直径85.3厘米，重5.6千克。器壁较薄，捶打制成，纹饰鎏金。

Dish with design of a phoenix (fragment)

Tang dynasty (618～907). Excavated at Hansenzhai, eastern suburbs of Xi'an city in 1956. Silver with gilding. Diameter: 85.3 cm, weight: 5600 g.

47 **鎏金“敬晦进”折枝团花纹五曲银碟**

唐(公元618～907年)。1958年春陕西省耀县柳林背阴村出土。高3.1厘米，直径17.6厘米，足径11.3厘米，重287克。盘底部錾刻“盐铁使臣敬晦进十二”9字。敬晦在唐宣宗大中年间（公元847～859年）先后官御史中丞、刑部侍郎、诸道盐铁转运使、浙江观察使等职。因此，银碟应是敬晦在当时进献给唐宣宗的贡品，“十二”是贡品的编号。

Dish with inscription of "*jing hui jin*"

Tang dynasty (618～907). Excavated at Beiyin village, Liulin, Yaoxian in 1958. Silver with gilding. Height: 3.1 cm, diameter of mouth: 17.6 cm, diameter of foot: 11.3 cm, weight: 287 g.

48A-B **鎏金鸿雁纹四曲银碟**

唐(公元618～907年)。1958年春陕西省耀县柳林背阴村出土。高4.5厘米，长18.1厘米，宽14.4厘米，重317克。侈口，浅腹，四曲海棠形口，椭圆形低圈足。捶打成型，内底錾刻鸿雁纹，纹饰鎏金，鱼子纹为地。从造型来看，应该是从萨珊式的银长杯演变而来的。

Four-lobed dish with design of wild geese

Tang dynasty (618～907). Excavated at Beiyin village, Liulin, Yaoxian in 1958. Silver with gilding. Height: 4.5 cm, length: 18.1 cm,width: 14.4 cm, weight: 317 g.

49 **五曲葵口银碟**

唐(公元618～907年)。1958年春陕西省耀县柳林背阴村出土。高1.8厘米，口径13.7厘米，重162克。

Five-lobed and sunflower-rimmed dish

Tang dynasty (618～907). Excavated at Beiyin village, Liulin, Yaoxian in 1958. Silver. Height: 1.8 cm, diameter: 13.7 cm, weight: 162 g.

50 **莲瓣形银茶托**

唐(公元618～907年)。1958年春陕西省耀县柳林背阴村出土。高3.1厘米，直径17.1厘米，重199克。为单瓣莲花形，捶打成型，通体光素。茶托是盛放茶杯的器具，相传为唐德宗时宰相崔宁之女创制，后流行于宫廷与贵族中。

Lotus-petal-shaped tea cup stand

Tang dynasty (618～907). Excavated at Beiyin village, Liulin, Yaoxian in 1958. Silver. Height: 3.1 cm, diameter: 17.1 cm, weight: 199 g.

51 **鎏金双鱼纹四曲银碟**

唐(公元618～907年)。1958年春陕西省耀县柳林背阴村出土。高5.2厘米，长15.5厘米，宽11.3厘米，重172克。

Four-lobed dish with design of two fish

Tang dynasty (618～907). Excavated at Beiyin village, Liulin, Yaoxian in 1958. Silver with gilding. Height: 5.2 cm, length: 15.5 cm, width: 11.3 cm, weight: 172 g.

52 **素面五尖瓣形银碟**

唐(公元618～907年)。1958年春陕西省耀县柳林背阴村出土。高1.4厘米，直径10厘米，重69克。

Five-petal-shaped dish

Tang dynasty (618～907). Excavated at Beiyin village, Liulin, Yaoxian in 1958. Silver. Height: 1.4 cm, diameter: 10 cm, weight: 69 g.

53 **素面海棠形银碟**

唐(公元618～907年)。1958年春陕西省耀县柳林背阴村出土。高1.3厘米，长14.2厘米，宽8.8厘米，重54克。

Chinese-flowering-crabapple-shaped dish

Tang dynasty (618～907). Excavated at Beiyin village, Liulin, Yaoxian in 1958. Silver. Height: 1.3 cm, length: 14.2 cm, width: 8.8 cm, weight: 54 g.

54 **鎏金“李杆进”鸳鸯绶带纹五曲银碟**

唐(公元618～907年)。1980年陕西省蓝田县汤峪杨家沟出土。高2.2厘米，直径20厘米，重265克。盘壁背面花纹与正面一致，盘底圈足内錾刻“桂管臣李杆进”6字，另刻有“七两半”、“捌两”、“捌”、“美”、“小贞”等字。

Dish with inscription of "*li gan jin*"

Tang dynasty (618～907). Excavated at Yangjiagou village, Lantian in 1980. Silver with gilding. Height: 2.2 cm, diameter: 20 cm, weight: 265 g.

55 **鎏金折枝花纹五曲银碟**

唐(公元618～907年)。1987年5月陕西省扶风县法门寺唐代地宫出土。高1.8厘米，口径11.1厘米，重124克。1991年5月从扶风县法门寺博物馆调拨。

Dish with design of floral sprays

Tang dynasty (618～907). Excavated from the crypt of Famen Temple, Fufeng in 1987. Silver with gilding. Height: 1.8 cm, diameter of mouth: 11.1 cm, weight: 124 g.

56 **双耳提梁银锅**

唐(公元618～907年)。1970年10月陕西省西安市南郊何家村基建工地唐代窖藏出土。高7.1厘米，口径19.2厘米，重740克。平折宽沿，敞口，直腹，圆底，捶打成型，通体经旋切、抛光处理。

Pot with two ears and an arc handle

Tang dynasty (618～907). Excavated at Hejiacun building site, southern suburbs of Xi’an city in 1970. Silver. Height: 7.1 cm, diameter of mouth: 19.2 cm, weight: 740 g.

57 **双耳提梁银锅**

唐(公元618～907年)。1970年10月陕西省西安市南郊何家村基建工地唐代窖藏出土。高4.2厘米，口径12.5厘米，重168克。

Pot with two ears and an arc handle

Tang dynasty (618～907). Excavated at Hejiacun building site, southern suburbs of Xi'an city in 1970. Silver. Height: 4.2 cm, diameter of mouth: 12.5 cm, weight: 168 g.

58 **双耳银锅**

唐(公元618～907年)。1970年10月陕西省西安市南郊何家村基建工地唐代窖藏出土。通高14厘米，口径28.2厘米，重1790克。锅为烹饪器，这件银锅可能是煎药用具，也有人认为是烹茶之器。

Pot with two ears and an arc handle

Tang dynasty (618～907). Excavated at Hejiacun building site, southern suburbs of Xi'an city in 1970. Silver. Height: 14 cm, diameter of mouth: 28.2 cm, weight: 1790 g.

59 **花叶形单柄银铛**

唐(公元618～907年)。1970年10月陕西省西安市南郊何家村基建工地唐代窖藏出土。高4.3厘米，口径10.5厘米，柄长2.5厘米，重148克。

Handled medicine warmer with three leaf-shaped feet

Tang dynasty (618～907). Excavated at Hejiacun building site, southern suburbs of Xi'an city in 1970. Silver. Height: 4.3 cm, diameter of mouth: 10.5 cm, length of handle: 2.5 cm, weight: 148g.

60 A-B **金药铫**

唐(公元618～907年)。1970年10月陕西省西安市南郊何家村基建工地唐代窖藏出土。高5.5厘米，口径14.5厘米，流长2.9厘米，重683克。内底墨书"旧泾用／十七两／暖药"3行8字，可知是温药之器。此器原定名单流金锅或金药铛，其实这种有柄有流的温器应名为铫，唐孙思邈《千金方》列的药具中就有铫，白居易《村居寄张殷衡》诗中有"药铫夜倾残酒暖"之句。

Medicine warmer

Tang dynasty (618～907). Excavated at Hejiacun building site, southern suburbs of Xi'an city in 1970. Gold. Height: 5.5 cm, diameter of mouth: 14.5 cm, weight: 683 g, length of spout: 2.9 cm.

61 A-C **双狮纹金铛**

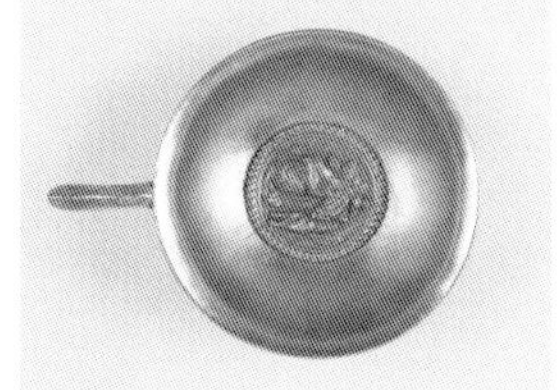

唐(公元618～907年)。1970年10月陕西省西安市南郊何家村基建工地唐代窖藏出土。高3.5厘米，口径9.2厘米，柄长2.9厘米，重268克。金铛为侈口、翻沿，圜底，三兽足，叶芽形单柄，捶打成型，花纹平錾，鱼子纹底纹。柄及兽足均焊接于腹上。器外底部中心分出9条水波纹曲线，将外壁划分为9个S形区间，内填以双鸟衔绶、双鸟衔方胜、立狮及花卉等纹饰。器内底饰高浮雕式的双狮相搏纹。从铛腹9个分区内及铛内底麦穗圆框中的立狮纹的作法来看，还有着较多的西方外来影响，但铛这种器形则是中国式的。铛在古代是炊器，唐代也用铛作煎药器具。道教炼丹术讲究使用金银制作的药具，这件金狮造型优美，制作精细，当是皇室使用的药具。

Medicine warmer with design of two lions

Tang dynasty (618～907). Excavated at Hejiacun building site, southern suburbs of Xi'an city in 1970. Gold. Height: 3.5 cm, diameter of mouth: 9.2 cm, length of handle: 2.9 cm, weight: 268 g.

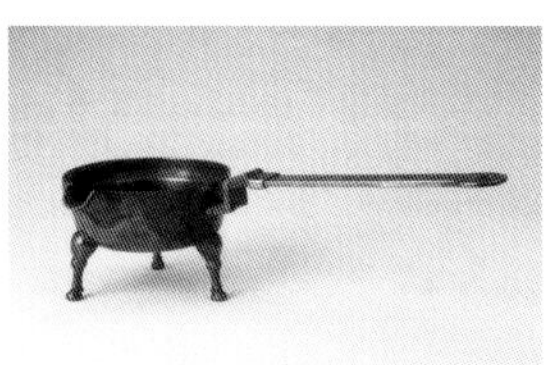

62 **单流折柄银铫**

唐(公元618～907年)。1970年10月陕西省西安市南郊何家村基建工地唐代窖藏出土。高7.7厘米，通长28.5厘米，口径10.5厘米，重519克。长柄与器身以活页相连，使用时打开，用柄上的游动套扣固定，不用时长柄可复原至器口，以节省体积。《卫生家室》讲五香连翘汤，须用银铫煎，可知银铫为温药、煎药之器。

Warmer with a spout and a folded handle

Silver. Tang dynasty (618～907). Excavated at Hejiacun building site, southern suburbs of Xi'an city in 1970. Height: 7.7 cm, diameter of mouth: 10.5 cm, total length: 28.5 cm, weight: 519 g.

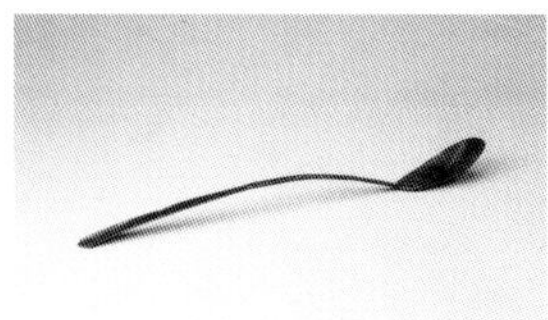

63 **银则**

唐(公元618～907年)。1955年陕西省西安市东郊韩森寨出土。长32.4厘米，最宽处4厘米，重83克。

Ladle

Tang dynasty (618～907). Excavated from a Tang tomb at Hansenzhai, eastern suburbs of Xi'an city in 1955. Silver. Length: 32.4 cm, the widest part: 4 cm, weight: 83 cm.

64 **银则（3件）**

唐(公元618～907年)。1958年陕西省西安市南郊姬家村出土。长19.1～19.4厘米，勺宽3.7～3.9厘米，重43～57克。

Ladles (3 pieces)

Tang dynasty (618～907). Excavated at Jijiacun, southern suburbs of Xi'an city in 1958. Silver. Length: 19.1～19.4 cm, width of spoon: 3.7～3.9 cm, weight: 43～ 57 g.

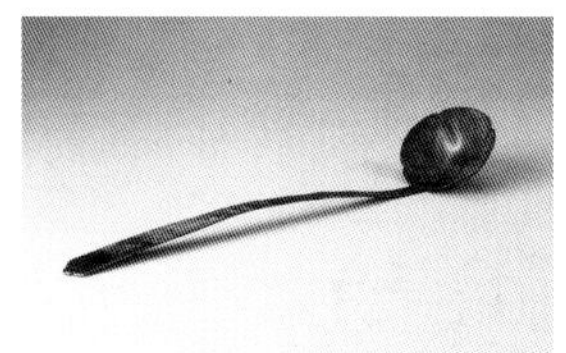

65 **四曲葵口银勺**

唐(公元618～907年)。1955年陕西省西安市东郊韩森寨出土。通长30.5厘米，勺口径7.8×6.8厘米，重116克。

Four-lobed and sunflower-rimmed ladle

Tang dynasty (618～907). Excavated from a Tang tomb at Hansenzhai, eastern suburbs of Xi'an city in 1955. Silver. Total length: 30.5 cm, size of spoon: 7.8 × 6.8 cm, weight: 116 g.

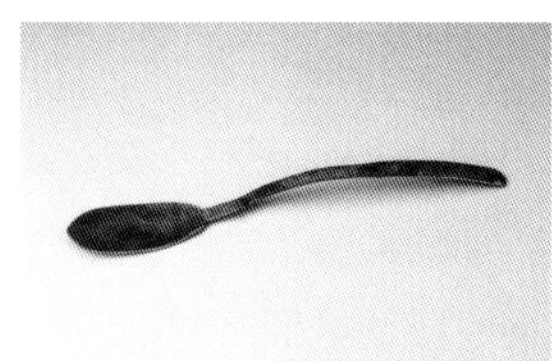

66 **鎏金花草纹银则**

唐(公元618～907年)。1958年陕西省耀县柳林背阴村出土。长27.7厘米，重71克。

Ladle with design of flowers and grass

Tang dynasty (618～907). Excavated at Beiyin village, Liulin, Yaoxian in 1958. Silver with gilding. Length: 27.7 cm, weight: 71 g.

67 **素面兽首衔环耳提梁银罐**

唐(公元618～907年)。1970年10月陕西省西安市南郊何家村基建工地唐代窖藏出土。器身高26.1厘米，盖高4.3厘米，口径16.9厘米，底径11.9厘米，重4150克。

Handled pot with a designed lid

Tang dynasty (618～907). Excavated at Hejiacun building site, southern suburbs of Xi'an city in 1970. Silver. Height of pot: 26.1 cm, height of lid: 4.3 cm, diameter of mouth: 16.9 cm, diameter of foot: 11.9 cm, weight: 4150 g.

68 鎏金鹦鹉纹提梁银罐

唐(公元618～907年)。1970年10月陕西省西安市南郊何家村基建工地唐代窖藏出土。通高24.1厘米，口径12厘米，重1879克。盖内面墨书“紫英五十两／石英十二两”2行10字。鹦鹉是能言之鸟，唐代宫廷贵族多喜养其珍贵品种，《明皇杂录》中就记载有唐玄宗所养白鹦鹉“雪衣娘”的故事，由于皇帝的喜好，鹦鹉成为画家笔下表现的对象，鹦鹉纹也成为各种器物装饰流行的题材。此罐以鹦鹉为中心，折枝花相缠绕，构成一幅生机盎然的画面，反映出唐人祈求康宁、幸福的美好愿望。盖内墨书表明此罐是用来贮放药物的。

Handled pot with design of parrots

Tang dynasty (618～907). Excavated at Hejiacun building site, southern suburbs of Xi'an city in 1970. Silver with gilding. Total height: 24.1 cm, diameter of mouth: 12 cm, weight: 1879 g.

69 素面提梁银盖罐

唐(公元618～907年)。1970年10月陕西省西安市南郊何家村基建工地唐代窖藏出土。通高12厘米，腹径11.2厘米，重387克。

Handled pot with a lid

Tang dynasty (618～907). Excavated at Hejiacun building site, southern suburbs of Xi'an city in 1970. Silver. Total height: 12 cm, diameter of belly: 11.2 cm, weight: 387 g.

70 素面平底银罐

唐(公元618～907年)。1970年10月陕西省西安市南郊何家村基建工地唐代窖藏出土。高4.1厘米，口径3.4厘米，重53克。

Pot with a flat base

Tang dynasty (618～907). Excavated at Hejiacun building site, southern suburbs of Xi'an city in 1970. Silver. Height: 4.1 cm, diameter of mouth: 3.4 cm, weight: 53 g.

71 素面直口银盖罐

唐(公元618～907年)。1970年10月陕西省西安市南郊何家村基建工地唐代窖藏出土。高7.5厘米，口径8.4厘米，底径6.3厘米，重429克。

Pot with an everted rim

Silver. Tang dynasty (618～907). Excavated at Hejiacun building site, southern suburbs of Xi'an city in 1970. Height:7.5cm, diameter of mouth: 8.4 cm, diameter of foot: 6.3 cm, weight: 429 g.

72 素面三足银罐

唐(公元618～907年)。1970年10月陕西省西安市南郊何家村基建工地唐代窖藏出土。

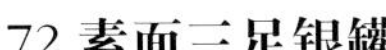

高4.7厘米，口径2.7厘米，重58克。小口，直领，鼓腹，小平底，宝珠钮盖与罐身以子母口相连。捶打成型，经旋切打磨，三足焊接器身。

Three-legged pot

Tang dynasty (618～907). Excavated at Hejiacun building site, southern suburbs of Xi'an city in 1970. Silver. Height: 4.7 cm, diameter of mouth: 2.7 cm, weight: 58 g.

73 素面三足束腰形银罐

唐(公元618～907年)。1970年10月陕西省西安市南郊何家村基建工地唐代窖藏出土。高3.8厘米，口径4.4厘米，重72克。

Three-legged pot with a concave waist

Tang dynasty (618～907). Excavated at Hejiacun building site, southern suburbs of Xi'an city

in 1970. Silver. Height: 3.8 cm, diameter of mouth: 4.4 cm, weight: 72 g.

74 **仰莲瓣座银罐**

唐(公元618～907年)。1970年10月陕西省西安市南郊何家村基建工地唐代窖藏出土。高11.4厘米，口径4厘米，腹径7.2厘米，重172克。

Pot with a lotus-petal-shaped base

Tang dynasty (618～907). Excavated at Hejiacun building site, southern suburbs of Xi'an city in 1970. Silver. Height: 11.4 cm, diameter of mouth: 4 cm, diameter of belly: 7.2 cm, weight: 172 g.

75 A-B **莲瓣纹提梁银罐**

唐(公元618～907年)。1970年10月陕西省西安市南郊何家村基建工地唐代窖藏出土。高20厘米，口径17.5厘米，足径15.3厘米，重1590克。盖内面六莲瓣内分别有墨书："珊瑚三段"、"琉璃杯碗各一"、"马脑(玛瑙)杯一"、"玉环一"、"玉臂杯四"、"颇黎(玻璃)"。从墨书内容可知罐内所放之物在唐时的名称，也可知此罐当时是用作储藏珍贵物品的容器。

Handled pot with design of lotus petals

Tang dynasty (618～907). Excavated at Hejiacun building site, southern suburbs of Xi'an city in 1970. Silver. Total height: 20 cm, diameter of mouth: 17.5 cm, diameter of foot: 15.3 cm, weight: 1590 g.

76 **鎏金春秋人物故事纹三足银罐**

唐(公元618～907年)。1958年春陕西省耀县柳林背阴村出土。高6.1厘米，口径3.3厘米，底径3.6厘米，重70克。腹部以凹棱分割出三个由众多人物组成的场景，旁有题榜，标明人物和故事，分别是"子路"、"灵公问政"、"少正卯"等，均取材于儒家经典，反映出晚唐时儒教对金银器的影响。

Three-legged jar with figures in landscape

Tang dynasty (618～907). Excavated at Beiyin village, Liulin, Yaoxian in 1958. Silver with gilding. Height: 6.1 cm, diameter of mouth: 3.3 cm, diameter of foot: 3.6 cm, weight: 70 g.

77 **银石榴罐**

唐(公元618～907年)。1970年10月陕西省西安市南郊何家村基建工地唐代窖藏出土。高9厘米，口外径2.5厘米，口内径1.7厘米，腹径6.1厘米，重851克。器体厚重，腹部有横向的焊接痕迹。据研究，这种银石榴罐是炼丹使用的。

Pomegranate-shaped pot

Tang dynasty (618～907). Excavated at Hejiacun building site, southern suburbs of Xi'an city in 1970. Silver. Height: 9 cm, diameter of outer mouth: 2.5 cm, diameter of inner mouth: 1.7 cm, weight: 851 g.

78 **银石榴罐**

唐(公元618～907年)。1970年10月陕西省西安市南郊何家村基建工地唐代窖藏出土。高9.6厘米，口外径2.7厘米，腹径6.2厘米，重899克。

Pomegranate-shaped pot

Tang dynasty (618～907). Excavated at Hejiacun building site, southern suburbs of Xi'an city in 1970. Silver. Height: 9.6 cm, diameter of outer mouth: 2.7 cm, diameter of belly: 6.2 cm, weight: 899 g.

79 **鎏金舞马衔杯纹银壶**

唐(公元618～907年)。1970年10月陕西省西安市南郊何家村基建工地唐代窖藏出土。高18.5厘米，口径2.3厘米，底足径8.9厘米×7.2厘米，重549克。银壶的造型为皮囊式，既便于外出骑猎携带，又便于日常生活使用，安全而卫生，设计上非常科学。在壶的两面采用点装手法各饰一匹奋首鼓尾、衔杯前拜的舞马。每年的阴历八月五日唐玄宗生日千秋节时，朝廷都要在兴庆宫的勤政务本楼下举行盛大的庆祝活动。在《倾杯乐》的乐曲中佩带金银珠宝的舞马翩翩起舞，"足踏天廷鼓舞，心将帝乐踟蹰"，"屈膝衔杯赴节，倾心献寿无疆"。擅长文辞，与苏颋一起被誉为"燕许大手笔"的宰相张说，曾这样描绘舞马："腕足徐行拜两膝，繁骄不进踏千蹄，……更有衔杯终宴曲，垂头掉尾醉如泥。"银壶上的舞马形象，表现的正是曲终衔杯祝寿这一独特的宫廷娱乐情景。

Flask with design of a dancing horse holding a cup in its mouth

Tang dynasty (618～907). Excavated at Hejiacun building site, southern suburbs of Xi'an city in 1970. Silver with gilding. Height 18.5 cm, diameter of mouth: 2.3 cm, size of foot: 8.9 cm × 7.2 cm, weight: 549 g.

80 **"宣徽酒坊"银酒注**

唐(公元618～907年)。1977年10月陕西省西安市西郊鱼化寨南二府庄出土。通高27.8厘米，口径14.1厘米，底径14厘米，流长7.9厘米，重3450克。银酒注为平底、圈足，肩部有对称系耳，提梁已失，杏叶形耳座，管状流。酒注外底錾刻文字7行61字："宣徽酒坊／咸通十三年六月二十日别敕造七升／地字号酒注壹枚重壹佰两匠／臣杨存实等造／监造蕃头品官冯金泰／都知高品臣张景谦／使高品臣宋师贞。"

Wine pitcther with inscription "*xuan hui jiu fang*"

Tang dynasty (618～907). Excavated at Erfuzhuang, Yuhuazhai, western suburbs of Xi'an city in 1977. Silver. Total height: 27.8 cm, diameter of mouth: 14.1 cm, diameter of foot: 14 cm, length of spout: 7.9 cm, weight: 3450 g.

81 **"大粒光明砂"银药盒**

唐(公元618～907年)。1970年10月陕西省西安市南郊何家村基建工地唐代窖藏出土。高6.5厘米，直径17.9厘米，盒重660克。盒盖内面墨书"大粒光明砂一大斤"等48字。何家村窖藏出土有一套金银药具，包括煎药的锅、铛，炼丹用的石榴罐，盛药的盒、罐，服药的碗、杯等，还有丹砂、乳石、琥珀、金屑等药物。唐代道教盛行，炼丹术发达，为了延年益寿、长生不老，达官显贵竞相服食金丹，连皇帝也笃信不疑，太宗、宪宗、穆宗、敬宗、武宗等皇帝的死亡，都与服食金丹有关。金银药盒上的墨书题记，或标明药名、服法，或记录重量，字迹至今仍清晰可辨，是研究中国古代医药发展的异常珍贵的实物资料。

Cinnabar box with inscription "*da li guang ming sha*" in black ink

Tang dynasty (618～907). Excavated at Hejiacun building site, southern suburbs of Xi'an city

in 1970. Silver. Height: 6.5 cm, diameter: 17.9 cm, weight: 660 g.

82 **“次光明砂”银药盒**

唐(公元618～907年)。1970年10月陕西省西安市南郊何家村基建工地唐代窖藏出土。高6.7厘米，直径15.6厘米，盒重1500克，内装朱砂444克，琥珀211克。盒内面墨书“合重卅六两”等17字。

Cinnabar box with inscription "*ci guang ming sha*" in black ink

Tang dynasty (618～907). Excavated at Hejiacun building site, southern suburbs of Xi'an city in 1970. Silver. Height: 6.7 cm, diameter: 15.6 cm, weight: 1500 g, cinnabar: 444 g, amber: 211 g.

83 **“红光丹砂”银药盒**

唐(公元618～907年)。1970年10月陕西省西安市南郊何家村基建工地唐代窖藏出土。高6.7厘米，直径17.4厘米，盒重674克。盒内面墨书“红光丹砂二大斤”等33字。丹砂又名朱砂、汞砂，中国第一部药书《神农本草经》将其列为上品。丹砂也是炼丹的主要药品，根据其形态、色泽又可分为许多等，最上者名光明砂，光明照彻，大小如豆者谓之豆砂，细赤碎者谓之碎砂。唐代，上好丹砂价格昂贵，且不易得到。

Cinnabar box with inscription "*hong guang dan sha*" in black ink

Tang dynasty (618～907). Excavated at Hejiacun building site, southern suburbs of Xi'an city in 1970. Silver. Height: 6.7 cm, diameter: 17.4 cm, weight: 674 g.

84 **“光明碎红砂”银药盒**

唐(公元618～907年)。1970年10月陕西省西安市南郊何家村基建工地唐代窖藏出土。高6.3厘米，直径17厘米，重668克。盒盖面及内面墨书“光明碎红砂”等39字。

Cinnabar box with inscription "*guang ming sui hong sha*" in black ink

Silver. Tang dynasty (618～907). Excavated at Hejiacun building site, southern suburbs of Xi'an city in 1970. Height: 6.3 cm, diameter: 17 cm, weight: 668 g.

85 **“光明紫砂”银药盒**

唐(公元618～907年)。1970年10月陕西省西安市南郊何家村基建工地唐代窖藏出土。高6.5厘米，直径17厘米，重648克。盒盖内面墨书“光明紫砂”等40字。

Cinnabar box with inscription "*guang ming zi sha*" in black ink

Tang dynasty (618～907). Excavated at Hejiacun building site, southern suburbs of Xi'an city in 1970. Silver. Height: 6.5 cm, diameter: 17 cm, weight: 648 g.

86 **“上上乳”银药盒**

唐(公元618～907年)。1970年10月陕西省西安市南郊何家村基建工地唐代窖藏出土。高6厘米，直径17.9厘米，盒重692克。盒盖墨书“上上乳一十八两”7字。

Box with inscription "*shang shang ru*" in black ink

Tang dynasty (618～907). Excavated at Hejiacun building site, southern suburbs of Xi'an city in 1970. Silver. Height: 6 cm, diameter: 17.9 cm, weight: 692 g .

87 **“次上乳”银药盒**

唐(公元618～907年)。1970年10月陕西省西安市南郊何家村基建工地唐代窖藏出土。高6.5厘米，直径17.4厘米，盒重675克。盒盖墨书“次上乳十四两三分堪服”10字。

Box with inscription "*ci shang ru*" in black ink

Tang dynasty (618～907). Excavated at Hejiacun building site, southern suburbs of Xi'an city in 1970. Silver. Height: 6.5 cm, diameter: 17.4 cm, weight: 675 g.

88A-B **“次乳”银药盒**

唐(公元618～907年)。1970年10月陕西省西安市南郊何家村基建工地唐代窖藏出土。高6.5厘米，直径17.95厘米，盒重655克。盒盖外面墨书“次乳廿四两”5字。盒盖内墨书“次乳廿四两／须简择／有堪服者”3行12字。石钟乳，又名芦石、鹅管石，《神农本草经》将其列为上品之药，此药也用于炼丹。从银盒墨书题记来看，唐代将石钟乳分为上上乳、次上乳、次乳三等。

Box with inscription "*ci ru*" in black ink

Tang dynasty (618～907). Excavated at Hejiacun building site, southern suburbs of Xi'an city in 1970. Silver. Height: 6.5 cm, diameter: 17.95 cm, weight: 655 g.

89 **素面金盒**

唐(公元618～907年)。1970年10月陕西省西安市南郊何家村基建工地唐代窖藏出土。高3.7厘米，直径8.5厘米，重259克。金盒先捶揲成型，然后再掏膛加工，在盒的内壁盖心处及底心处，旋切遗留下来的走刀痕迹非常清晰，排列密集，同心圆度强，起刀和落刀点也能看得清清楚楚。盒身上下以子母口相扣，无论怎样转动，扣合得都严丝合缝。出土时金盒内放有麸金，麸金是从沙土中淘拣出来的金屑，因小如麸皮，故名麸金。麸金属砂金，是中国古代黄金的主要来源。据《新唐书·地理志》记载，当时向朝廷进贡麸金的地区有涪州、金州等30多处。唐人信奉道教，认为服食金屑可轻身不老，麸金也是送人的贵重礼物。唐代麸金，这是唯一的一次发现。盒盖内心墨书“六两一分”4字。

Box

Tang dynasty (618～907年). Excavated at Hejiacun building site, southern suburbs of Xi'an city in 1970. Gold. Height: 3.7 cm, diameter: 8.5 cm, weight: 259 g.

90 **鎏金宝相花纹银盒**

唐(公元618～907年)。1970年10月陕西省西安市南郊何家村基建工地出土。高2.6厘米，直径8.7厘米，重161克。

Box with design of lotus medallions

Tang dynasty (618～907). Excavated at Hejiacun building site, southern suburbs of Xi'an city in 1970. Silver with gilding. Height: 2.6 cm, diameter: 8.7 cm, weight: 161 g.

91A-C **鎏金石榴花结纹银盒**

唐(公元618～907年)。1970年10月陕西省西安市南郊何家村基建工地唐代窖藏出土。高6.6厘米，直径12.8厘米，重414克。盖内面墨书“十两／溪州丹砂卅七两／兼盛黄粉”。盒身分五层装饰图案，中心是一朵八出团花，外绕一重石榴花结，再间隔一周荷叶状花结，外圈是柿状花结组成的六出团花八朵分布在盒沿。在银盒侧面上下都有半朵柿形花组成的团花，当盒沿对准扣合时就是一朵完整的团花，花纹细密精美，为满地装之杰作。石榴多子，唐人常常用来象征子孙繁衍、人丁兴旺，这件银盒纹饰虽然繁复细密，但却井然有序，显得典雅富丽，洋溢着盛唐文化的神韵。唐代银盒作为精

致的小型容器，它的用途是多种多样的，道家术士，讲究用银盒盛放丹药，认为以银为器可以养丹砂。银盒也是皇宫中常用之物，《太平广记》卷221记述了这样一则有趣的故事：袁天纲之子袁客师精通方术，有一次，唐高宗为了考察一下方士们的水平，将一只老鼠放在银盒中，让方士们猜有几只，其他方士都说一只，唯独袁客师说："鼠也，然入一出四"结果竟然猜对，原来老鼠进入银盒后又生三鼠，袁客师由此也出了名。

Box with design of pomegranate-flower-knots

Tang dynasty (618～907). Excavated at Hejiacun building site, southern suburbs of Xi'an city in 1970. Silver with gilding. Height: 6.6 cm, diameter: 12.8 cm, weight: 414 g.

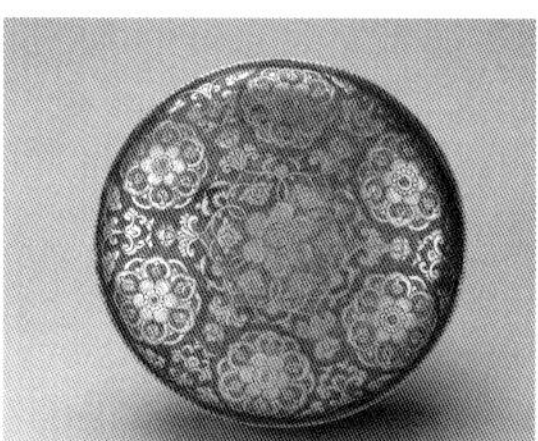

92A-C **鎏金飞狮纹银盒**

唐(公元618～907年)。1970年10月陕西省西安市南郊何家村基建工地唐代窖藏出土。高5.6厘米，直径12.9厘米，重425克。银盒为圆形，盒盖与底面稍稍隆起，中部平坦，上下以子母口相扣合。银盒捶打成型后，又经切削、打磨处理，修整得圆润、光滑。盒内面有清晰的旋切留下的刀纹，间距仅1毫米。纹饰以鱼子纹为底，盖面在麦穗纹圆形框架中，錾刻出一只张动鬣毛、飞扬双翼的狮子，周围绕以六朵宝相花组成的折枝花，盖底中心，錾刻一朵六瓣团花，绕以六出石榴花结，盒沿则錾刻出六组形态各异的飞禽走兽，间以折枝花草。纹饰全部鎏金，黄白辉映，煜煜夺目。萨珊和粟特的金银器上的动物，多为想像出的带有双翼的神异形象，并在周围加一麦穗纹圆框，学者称其为"徽章式纹样"。这件银盒上飞狮纹构图显然是接受了萨珊艺术的影响。银盒不仅用来盛放丹药，也用来盛放贵重的化妆品，口脂、面药、衣香、澡豆是唐代贵族喜用的美容化妆品，每逢腊日，皇帝便将金银盒及化妆品分赐将相大臣。张九龄在《为郭令公谢腊日赐香药表》里，就提到有"金花银盒子两枚、面脂一盒"。杜甫《腊日》诗中有："口脂面药随恩泽，翠管银罂下九霄。"

Box with design of a flying lion

Tang dynasty (618～907). Excavated at Hejiacun building site, southern suburbs of Xi'an city in 1970. Silver with gilding. Height: 5.6 cm, diameter: 12.9 cm, weight: 425 g.

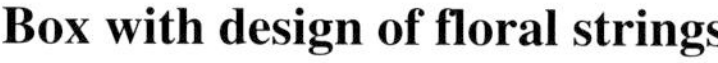

93A-B **鎏金宝相串枝花纹银盒**

唐(公元618～907年)。1970年10月陕西省西安市南郊何家村基建工地唐代窖藏出土。高4.7厘米，直径11.4厘米，重290克。银盒为六曲花形，盒盖与底面隆起较高，中部平坦，上下以子母口相扣合，合缝严密，无法转动。盒面主题纹饰已由萨珊式的圆框中的动物变为唐代流行的宝相花类。刘禹锡在《谢敕书赐腊日口脂等表》里讲皇帝腊日所赐物有"面脂、口脂、红雪、紫雪，并金花银盒二、金棱盒二"。棱盒应当就是这种多曲花瓣形的盒子。

Box with design of floral strings

Tang dynasty (618～907). Excavated at Hejiacun building site, southern suburbs of Xi'an city in 1970. Silver with gilding. Height: 4.7 cm, diameter: 11.4 cm, weight: 290 g.

94 **鎏金线刻凤鸟纹银盒**

唐(公元618～907年)。1970年10月陕西省西安市南郊何家村基建工地唐代窖藏出土。通高2.9厘米，直径8.3厘米，重182克。盒盖面用阴线刻划出展翅欲飞的凤凰，线条流畅、细腻，风格简洁明快，为唐代金银器装饰所罕见之手法。

Box with design of phoenixes

Tang dynasty (618～907). Excavated at Hejiacun building site, southern suburbs of Xi'an city in 1970. Silver with gilding. Height: 2.9 cm, diameter: 8.3 cm, weight: 182 g.

95 **鎏金刻花小银盒**

唐(公元618～907年)。1970年10月陕西省西安市南郊何家村基建工地唐代窖藏出土。通高2厘米，直径4.1厘米，重49克。盒上下内面有密集的、间距在0.5～1毫米的同心圆细线，盖面有细如发丝的线刻花纹，起刀、落刀痕迹明显。叶子中间用刻刀来回划刻，似平涂，以造出叶子的效果。

Box with design of engraved flowers

Tang dynasty (618～907). Excavated at Hejiacun building site, southern suburbs of Xi'an city in 1970. Silver with gilding. Height: 2 cm, diameter: 4.1 cm, weight: 49 g.

96 **鎏金鸳鸯纹小银盒**

唐(公元618～907年)。1970年10月陕西省西安市南郊何家村基建工地唐代窖藏出土。高1.9厘米，直径4.2厘米，重36克。

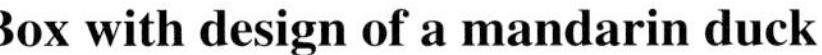

Box with design of a mandarin duck

Tang dynasty (618～907). Excavated at Hejiacun building site, southern suburbs of Xi'an city in 1970. Silver with gilding. Height: 1.9 cm, diameter: 4.2 cm, weight: 36 g.

97A-B **鎏金仙鹤翼鹿纹银盒**

唐(公元618～907年)。1970年10月陕西省西安市南郊何家村基建工地唐代窖藏出土。高2厘米，直径4.8厘米，重56克。盒盖中央在麦穗圆框中，錾刻一朵双层八瓣团花，外围绕以四只仙鹤与四朵莲叶卷草相间组成的花鸟图案，盒底中央圆框中錾刻一只口衔瑞草、身生双翼的鹿，外绕八朵忍冬花结。通体以鱼子纹为底纹，纹饰全部鎏金。有趣的是，这件银盒虽然在纹饰构图上还有萨珊影响，但却将唐时流行的团花纹放在主要位置，外来影响明显的翼鹿纹放在次要位置。

Box with design of cranes and a winged deer

Tang dynasty (618～907). Excavated at Hejiacun building site, southern suburbs of Xi'an city in 1970. Silver with gilding. Height: 2 cm, diameter: 4.8 cm, weight: 56 g.

98A-B **鎏金翼鹿凤鸟纹银盒**

唐(公元618～907年)。1970年10月陕西省西安市南郊何家村基建工地唐代窖藏出土。高2.4厘米，直径6厘米，重62克。盖和底两面均稍隆起，子母口相扣合。盖面中央錾刻一口衔绶带的双翼平角牡鹿，周围为八朵莲叶忍冬组成的石榴花结，盖底中央錾刻一口衔绶带的凤鸟，周边为八朵桃形忍冬花结。构图方式还可看出萨珊艺术的影响。

Box with design of a winged deer and a phoenix

Tang dynasty (618～907). Excavated at Hejiacun building site, southern suburbs of Xi'an city in 1970. Silver with gilding. Height: 2.4 cm, diameter: 6 cm, weight: 62 g.

99A-B **鎏金双鸾纹银盒**

唐(公元618～907年)。1970年10月陕西省西安市南郊何家村基建工地唐代窖藏出土。高1.4厘米，直径4.1厘米，重40克。盒盖面纹饰为双鸾衔方胜绶带，站立在莲蓬之上，双鸾作展翅欲飞状。盒底面纹饰为四朵桃形花结伸展出去的莲花，其间插以莲蓬。整

个纹饰流畅活泼，已为浓郁的中国风格。

Box with design of two phoenix-looking birds

Tang dynasty (618～907). Excavated at Hejiacun building site, southern suburbs of Xi'an city in 1970. Silver with gilding. Height: 1.4 cm, diameter: 4.1 cm, weight: 40 g.

100 **素面银盒**

唐(公元618～907年)。1970年10月陕西省西安市南郊何家村基建工地唐代窖藏出土。高3.7厘米，直径8.8厘米，重245克。

Box

Tang dynasty (618～907). Excavated at Hejiacun building site, southern suburbs of Xi'an city in 1970. Silver. Height: 3.7 cm, diameter: 8.8 cm, weight: 245 g.

101 **鎏金串枝花纹银盒**

唐(公元618～907年)。1970年10月陕西省西安市南郊何家村基建工地唐代窖藏出土。高3.7厘米，直径7.5厘米，重146克。

Box with design of floral strings

Tang dynasty (618～907). Excavated at Hejiacun building site, southern suburbs of Xi'an city in 1970. Silver. Height: 3.7 cm, diameter: 7.5 cm, weight: 146 g.

102A-B **鎏金犀牛石榴花纹银盒**

唐(公元618～907年)。1970年10月陕西省西安市南郊何家村基建工地唐代窖藏出土。高2.5厘米，直径5.8厘米，重108克。

Box with design of a rhino and pomegranate flowers

Tang dynasty (618～907). Excavated at Hejiacun building site, southern suburbs of Xi'an city in 1970. Silver with gilding. Height: 2.5 cm, diameter: 5.8 cm, weight: 108 g.

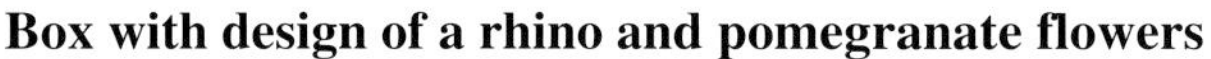

103 **素面银盒**

唐(公元618～907年)。1964年12月陕西省长安县天子峪国清寺塔出土。高4.9厘米，直径5.6厘米，重55克。

Box

Tang dynasty (618～907). Excavated from the crypt of Guoqing temple, Chang'an in 1964. Silver. Height: 4.9 cm, diameter: 5.6 cm, weight: 55 g.

104 **鎏金花鸟纹双层银盒**

唐(公元618～907年)。1955年2月陕西省西安市西郊土门唐墓出土。长4厘米，宽2.6厘米，高2.7厘米，重19克。这种双层银盒在目前发现的唐代金银器中还较为少见。

Two-layered box with design of flowers and birds

Tang dynasty (618～907). Excavated from a Tang tomb at Tumen, western suburbs of Xi'an city in 1955. Silver with gilding. Length: 4 cm, width: 2.6 cm, height: 2.7 cm, weight: 19 g.

105 **鎏金鹦鹉纹云头形银粉盒**

唐(公元618～907年)。1955年陕西省西安市文管会移交。通高3厘米，长10.6厘米，宽5.8厘米，重102克。

Cloud-head-shaped powder box with design of parrots

Tang dynasty (618～907). Handed in by the Cultural Relics Committee of Xi'an City in 1955. Silver with gilding. Total height: 3 cm, length: 10.6 cm, width: 5.8 cm, weight: 102 g.

106 **鎏金鹦鹉卷草纹云头形银粉盒（2件）**

唐(公元618～907年)。1980年陕西省蓝田县汤峪杨家沟出土。1991年4月从蓝田县文管会调拨。其一高3.4厘米，长9.7厘米，宽6.1厘米，重90克；其二高3.5厘米，长9.6厘米，宽5.9厘米，重86克。粉是唐代妇女常用的化妆品，有银(白)粉、红粉、胡粉等。盛放粉的盒亦有用金、银、玉、瓷、蚌等材料制作的，造型也多种多样。

Cloud-head-shaped powder box with design of parrots and vine scrolls (2 pieces)

Tang dynasty (618～907). Excavated at Yangjiagou, Tangyu, Lantian in 1980. Handed in by the Cultural Relics Committee of Lantian County in 1991. Silver with gilding. Total height: 3.4～3.5 cm, length: 9.6～ 9.7 cm, width: 5.9～6.1 cm, weight: 86～ 90 g.

107 **鎏金蝴蝶纹海棠形银盒**

唐(公元618～907年)。1955年陕西省西安市东郊纬十八街唐墓出土。长5厘米，宽3.4厘米，高2.2厘米，重18克。

Chinese-flowering-crabapple-shaped box with design of butterflies

Tang dynasty (618～907). Excavated at Weishiba street, eastern suburbs of Xi'an city in 1955. Silver with gilding. Length: 5 cm, width: 3.4 cm, height: 2.2 cm, weight: 18 g.

108 **金襟钩**

春秋(公元前770年～公元前476年)。1986年陕西省凤翔县秦公一号大墓出土。1991年4月从陕西省考古所雍城考古工作队调拨。高1.4厘米，长2.1厘米，宽1.8厘米，重19克。中空，壁厚仅0.1厘米，为浇铸成型。鸭头部用阴线刻出嘴、眼的细部。

Robe hook

Spring and Autumn period (770～476 B.C.). Excavated from the tomb of Duke Qin, Fengxiang. Allocated from Yongcheng Archaeological Station of Shaanxi Archaeological Institute in 1991. Gold. Height: 1.4 cm, length: 2.1 cm, width: 1.8 cm, weight: 19 g.

109 **盘羊形银扣饰**

战国(公元前475年～公元前221年)。1957年秋陕西省神木县纳林高兔村出土。1991年3月从神木县文管会调拨。高2.1厘米，长4.2厘米，重21克。与银虎、金鹿形怪兽同出一墓，为匈奴人遗物。

Coiled-goat-shaped buckle

Warring States period (475～221 B.C.). Excavated at Gaotu village, Nalin, Shenmu. Allocated from the Cultural Relics Committee of Shenmu County in 1991. Silver. Height: 2.1 cm, length: 4.2 cm, weight: 21 g.

110 **金耳坠（1对）**

西周（公元前1046年～公元前771年）。1982年12月陕西省淳化县西周早期墓出土。1991年3月从淳化县文化馆调拨。其一长7.4厘米，宽6.6厘米，厚0.04厘米，重10克；其二长7.3厘米，宽5.5厘米，厚0.03厘米，重8克。金耳坠为圆柱形曲柄，扁平螺旋式花头，捶打制成，薄厚均匀，表面光滑平坦，光洁度非常好。这种造型的金耳坠，在山西石楼的后兰家沟、桃花庄、永和的下辛角，陕西清涧的寺嫣村、淳化的黑豆嘴塬等地的墓葬中均有发现，有的还与男子使用的兵器同出，因此推断，金耳坠是男子戴的饰物。

Earrings (a pair)

Early Western Zhou Dynasty (1046～771 B.C.). Excavated from an early Western Zhou tomb, Chunhua. Transferred from the Cultural Center of Chunhua County in 1991. Gold. Length: 7.3～7.4 cm, thickness: 0.03～0.04 cm,weight: 8～10 g.

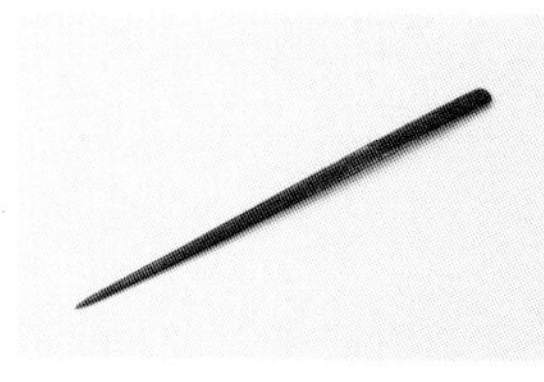

111 **鎏金飞鸟纹银簪**

唐(公元618～907年)。1956年陕西省西安市东郊韩森寨唐墓出土。长14.3厘米，重14克。

Hairpin with design of flying birds

Tang dynasty (618～907). Excavated at Hansenzhai, eastern suburbs of Xi'an city in 1956. Silver with gilding. Length: 14.3 cm, weight: 14 g.

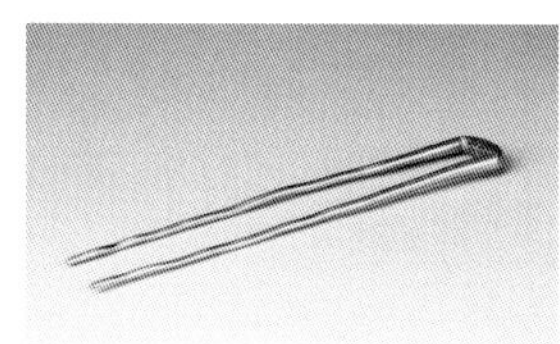

112 **素面金钗**

唐(公元618～907年)。1973年陕西省西安市仪表厂窑场出土。长10厘米，宽1.6厘米，重14克。

Hairpin

Tang dynasty (618～907). Excavated at the kiln site of Xi'an Instrument and Meter Plant in 1973. Gold. Length: 10 cm, width: 1.6 cm, weight: 14 g.

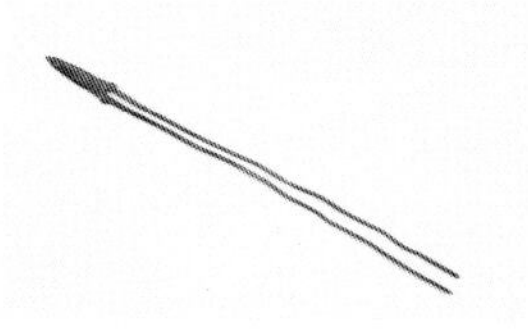

113 **花苞头银钗**

唐(公元618～907年)。1955年陕西省户县出土。通长27.1厘米，重30克。

Hairpin with a flower-bud-shaped final

Tang dynasty (618～907). Excavated in Huxian in 1955. Silver. Total length: 27.1 cm, weight: 30 g.

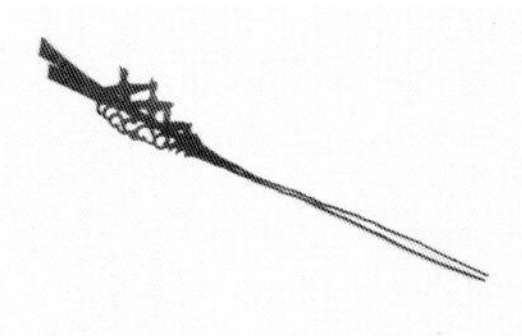

114 **鎏金鸿雁纹银钗**

唐(公元618～907年)。1952年陕西省博物馆收购吴云樵旧藏。通长29.5厘米，最宽处6厘米，重17克。

Hairpin with design of wild geese

Tang dynasty (618～907). Purchased by Shaanxi Provincial Museum in 1952. Silver with gilding. Total length: 29.5 cm, the widest part: 6 cm, weight: 17 g.

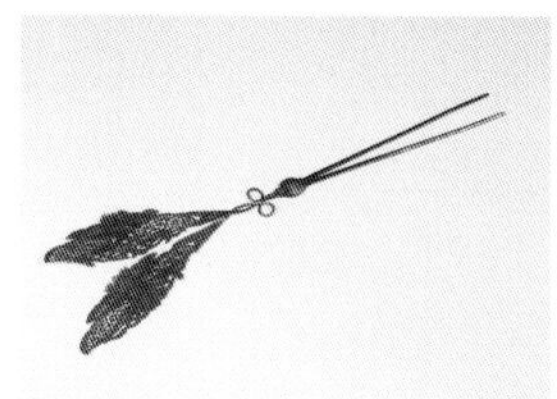

115 **鎏金蝴蝶纹银钗**

唐(公元618～907年)。1956年陕西省西安市东郊韩森寨唐墓出土。长35.4厘米，最宽处9.6厘米，重37克。

Hairpin with openwork design of butterflies

Tang dynasty (618～907). Excavated at Hansenzhai, eastern suburbs of Xi'an city in 1956. Silver with gilding. Length: 35.4 cm, the widest part: 9.6 cm, weight: 37 g.

116 鎏金菊花纹银钗（2件）

唐(公元618～907年)。1952年陕西省博物馆收购吴云樵旧藏。其一残长29.8厘米，最宽处7.5厘米，重30克；其二长34.5厘米，最宽处7.5厘米，重30克。钗是古代妇女用以绾发的一种装饰，一般由两股合成。唐代贵族妇女流行云鬟高髻，讲究发髻的造型，头部装饰复杂华丽，出现用金银制作的各种花钗。唐代的花钗，一般为一式两件，构图相同，图案向相反，使用时，左右对称地插戴在发髻两旁。花钗的使用有着严格的等级规定，《新唐书·车服志》记载，命妇之服，一品花钗九树，二品花钗八树，三品花钗七树，四品花钗六树，五品花钗五树。妇人头上花钗的多少，成为其身份高低的重要标志。

Hairpins with openwork design of chrysanthemums (2 pieces)

Tang dynasty (618～907). Purchased by Shaanxi Provincial Museum in 1952. Silver with gilding. Total length: 29.8～34.5 cm, the widest part: 7.5 cm, weight: 30 g.

117 鎏金摩羯莲叶纹银钗（2件）

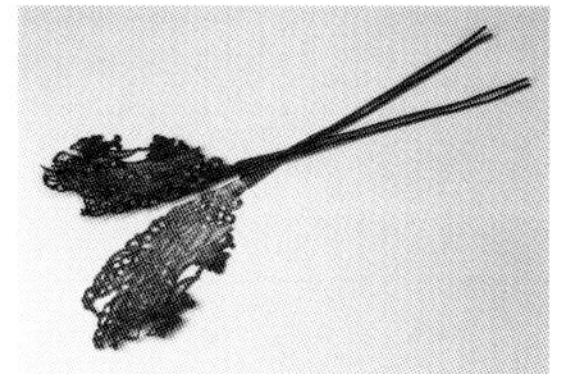

唐(公元618～907年)。1952年陕西省博物馆收购吴云樵旧藏。其一长35厘米，最宽处8厘米，重34.5克；其二长35厘米，最宽处8厘米，重35克。

Hairpin with openwork design of Makara and lotus leaves (2 pieces)

Tang dynasty (618～907). Purchased by Shaanxi Provincial Museum in 1952. Silver with openwork gilding. Total length: 35 cm, the widest part: 8 cm, weight: 34.5～35 g.

118 鎏金伽陵频嘉纹银钗

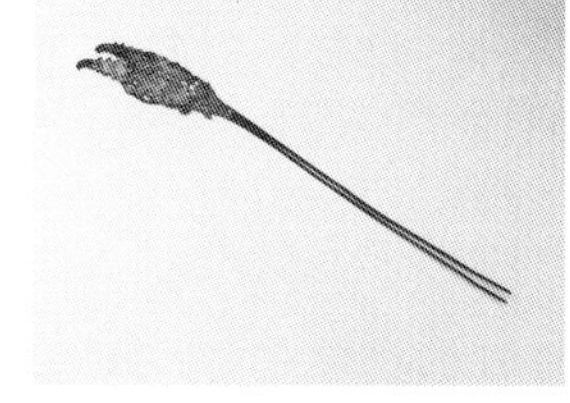

唐(公元618～907年)。1952年陕西省博物馆收购吴云樵旧藏。长30.5厘米，最宽处3.8厘米，重13克。伽陵频嘉，梵语kaiarinka，意译好声鸟、美音鸟，此鸟产于印度，色黑似雀，羽毛甚美，在佛教中谓此鸟即极乐净土之鸟，在净土曼荼罗中，作人头鸟身形。

Hairpin with openwork design of Kalavinkas

Tang dynasty (618～907). Purchased by Shaanxi Provincial Museum in 1952. Silver with gilding. Total length: 30.5 cm, the widest part: 3.8 cm, weight: 13 g.

119 鎏金银蝴蝶形头饰

唐(公元618～907年)。1956年陕西省西安市东郊韩森寨唐墓出土。长6.6厘米，最宽处3厘米，重2克。《开元天宝遗事》记载，唐玄宗时，后宫嫔妃争相求宠，为此，“明皇每至春时旦暮，宴于宫中，使嫔妃辈争插艳花，帝亲捉粉蝶放之，随蝶所止幸之。后因杨妃专宠，遂不复此戏也。”将头饰做成栩栩如生的蝴蝶形，大概是这种习俗影响所致吧！

Hairpin in the shape of a butterfly

Tang dynasty (618～907). Excavated from a Tang tomb at Hansenzhai, eastern suburbs of Xi'an city in 1956. Silver with gilding. Total length: 6.6 cm, the widest part: 3 cm, weight: 2 g.

120 金筐宝钿鸿雁衔枝纹金梳背

唐(公元618～907年)。1956年陕西省西安市东郊韩森寨唐墓出土。高1.8厘米，长7.5厘米，厚0.16厘米，重2克。唐代贵族妇女多喜欢在发髻上插上用金或玉制作的小梳子作装饰，王建《宫词》中的“玉蝉金雀三层插，翠髻高耸绿鬟虚。舞处春风吹落地，归来别赐一头梳”就形象地描绘出妇女发髻优美的造型和复杂的装饰。元稹的《恨梳成》中也有“满头行小梳，当面施圆靥”之句。

Comb-back with filigree design of wild geese holding floral sprays in their mouths

Tang dynasty (618～907). Excavated at Hansenzhai, eastern suburbs of Xi'an city in 1956. Gold with pearl inlays. Height: 1.8 cm, Length: 7.5 cm, thickness: 0.16 cm, weight: 2 g.

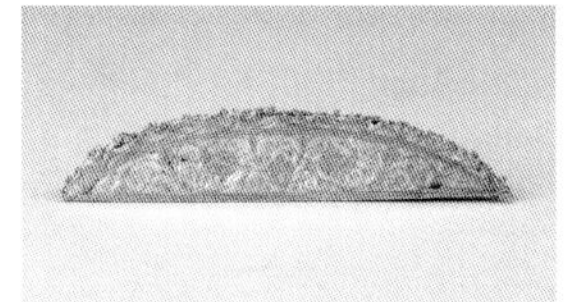

121 **金筐宝钿卷草纹金梳背**

唐(公元618～907年)。1970年10月陕西省西安市南郊何家村基建工地唐代窖藏出土。高1.7厘米，长7.2厘米，厚0.05厘米，重3克。金梳背中空，用0.05厘米厚的金箔压印出卷草花纹，纹饰内填以小金珠，弧形顶部有用金丝缠绕成的花纹。

Comb-back with floral design

Tang dynasty (618～907). Excavated at Hejiacun building site, southern suburbs of Xi'an city in 1970. Gold. Length: 7.2 cm, height: 1.7 cm, thickness: 0.05 cm, weight: 3 g.

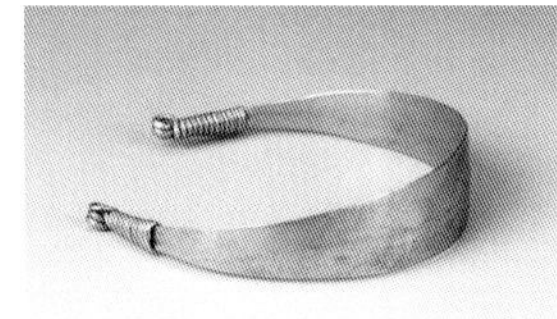

122 **金臂钏**

唐(公元618～907年)。1970年10月陕西省西安市南郊何家村基建工地唐代窖藏出土。最宽处1.7厘米，重33克。臂钏又称臂环，金臂钏是唐代皇室贵族妇女臂上戴的饰物，《明皇杂录》记唐玄宗时曾赐女伶粟妆金臂环，《卢氏杂说》记唐文宗赐宫人沈翘翘金臂环。

Armlet

Tang dynasty (618～907). Excavated at Hejiacun building site, southern suburbs of Xi'an city in 1970. Gold. The widest part: 1.7 cm, weight: 33 g.

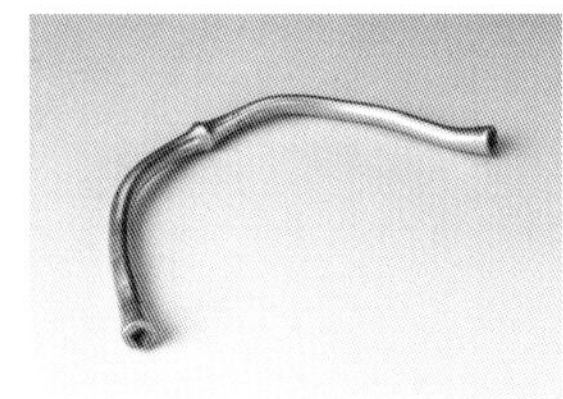

123 **竹节形金手镯**

唐(公元618～907年)。1970年10月陕西省西安市南郊何家村基建工地唐代窖藏出土。长19.5厘米，最大径0.95厘米，重111克。由于挤压，金手镯已严重变形。

Bamboo-joint-shaped bracelet

Tang dynasty (618～907). Excavated at Hejiacun building site, southern suburbs of Xi'an city in 1970. Gold. The biggest diameter: 0.95 cm, length: 19.5 cm, weight: 111 g.

124 **鎏金龙纹银带銙**

明(公元1368～1644年)。1956年5月陕西省西安市徐家堡明墓出土。长11～3.4厘米，重125克。

Belt plaques with design of dragons

Ming dynasty (1368～1644). Excavated from a Ming dynasty tomb, Xujiabu village, Xi'an city in 1956. Silver with gilding. Length: 11～3.4 cm, weight: 125 g.

125A-B **鎏金铜佛像**

东魏(公元534～550年)。2000年陕西省西安市未央区大刘寨村出土。高35厘米，底座径11厘米，背光宽15.5厘米，重2730克。底座正中处錾刻“比丘惠津敬造供养”8字。由主尊、背屏、左右胁侍菩萨、底座、左右翼形饰件7部分组成。法相庄严肃穆，制作工艺精湛，与山东青州龙兴寺遗址出土的北魏晚期至东魏时期的石刻佛教造像相接近。

Statue of Buddha

Eastern Wei dynasty (534～550). Excavated in Weiyang district, Xi'an city in 2000. Gilded bronze. Height: 35 cm, diameter of base: 11 cm, width of flaming haloes: 15.5 cm, weight: 2730 g.

126 银力士像

唐(公元618～907年)。1955年7月陕西省西安市文管会移交。高20.8厘米，宽6.5厘米，重89克。力士头戴宝冠，上身穿明光铠，披宝缯，腰系绦带，身穿战裙，着长靴，脚踏束腰形座。两眼圆睁，双手执兵器，充满威风凛凛的气势。

Statue of Vajrapani

Tang dynasty (618～907). Handed in by the Cultural Relics Committee of Xi'an city in 1955. Silver. Height: 20.8 cm, width: 6.5 cm, weight: 89 g.

127 银力士像

唐(公元618～907年)。1955年7月陕西省西安市文管会移交。高22.8厘米，宽6.1厘米，重100克。力士头戴宝冠，上身穿明光铠，披宝缯，腰系绦带，身穿战裙，着长靴，脚踏束腰形座。两眼圆睁，左手插腰，右手执举兵器。

Statue of Vajrapani

Tang dynasty (618～907). Handed in by the Cultural Relics Committee of Xi'an city in 1955. Silver. Height: 22.8 cm, width: 6.1 cm, weight: 100 g.

128 银力士像

唐(公元618～907年)。1955年7月陕西省西安市文管会移交。高17.5厘米，宽6.5厘米，重77克。力士头戴宝冠，上身穿明光铠，披宝缯，腰系绦带，身穿成裙，着长靴，脚踏底座。两眼圆睁，右手执武器插于腰间，左手上举于胸前，整体比例匀称，装饰细腻。

Statue of Vajrapani

Tang dynasty (公元 618～907). Handed in by the Cultural Relics Committee of Xi'an city in 1955. Silver. Height: 17.5 cm, width: 6.5 cm, weight: 77 g.

129 **银力士像**

唐(公元618～907年)。1955年7月陕西省西安市文管会移交。高17.5厘米，宽6.6厘米，重81克。力士头戴宝冠，上身穿明光铠，披宝缯，腰系绦带，身穿战裙，着长靴，脚踏底座。两眼圆睁，右手执武器支于地面，左手插腰，勇猛之气十足。

Statue of Vajrapani

Tang dynasty (618～907). Handed in by the Cultural Relics Committee of Xi'an city in 1955. Silver. Height: 17.5 cm, width: 6.6 cm, weight: 81 g.

130 **银力士像**

唐(公元618～907年)。1955年7月陕西省西安市文管会移交。高16.6厘米，宽7.3厘米，重57克。造型与前一银力士类似，只是脚下无踏座。这一组银力士像从造型来看，似乎是佛教用物上的装饰附件。

Statue of Vajrapani

Tang dynasty (618～907). Handed in by the Cultural Relics Committee of Xi'an city in 1955. Silver. Height: 16.6 cm, width: 7.3 cm, weight: 57 g.

131 **鎏金孔雀纹盝顶银宝函**

唐(公元618～907年)。1970年10月陕西省西安市南郊何家村基建工地唐代窖藏出土。高10厘米，边长12厘米，重1500克。宝函的正面錾刻一对振翅扬尾、立于莲座之上的孔雀，辅衬以山峰、花鸟、流云、芳草，其余各面也都是采用平视式纹样，把人物、风景、花鸟巧妙地结合起来，具有浓郁的大自然气息，反映出盛唐时期人们热爱自然、注重环境的思想意识。盖与器身用合页相连，并可上锁。

Cube-shaped casket with design of peacocks

Tang dynasty (618～907). Excavated at Hejiacun building site, southern suburbs of Xi'an city in 1970. Silver with gilding. Height: 10 cm, side length: 12 cm, weight: 1500 g.

132A-D **鎏金兔纹盝顶银宝函**

辽(公元907～1125年)。1993年法国收藏家克里斯蒂安·戴狄安捐赠。高6.8厘米，底边7.4厘米，重713克。银函为正方形，盝形顶。盒壁四周均錾刻一对振翅扬尾的凤，周围填以流云纹，盖顶捶打出一只鼓目扬首的兔纹，周围錾刻回旋式缠枝花纹。鱼子纹作底纹，主题纹饰全部鎏金。函内底錾刻“睿文英武尊道至德文忠王府祭器太平六年吉日造成又贡”24字。太平是辽圣宗耶律隆绪的年号，太平六年即公元1026年。关于文忠王府，《辽史·营卫志》记载：“大丞相晋国王耶律隆运，本韩氏，名德让。以功赠国姓，出宫籍，隶横帐季父房。赠尚书令，谥文忠。……宫给葬具，建庙乾陵侧。拟诸宫例，建文忠王府。……州一，提辖司六：上京、中京、南京、西京、奉圣州、平州。”在六个地方建文忠王府，作为祭器之一的这件银宝函到底应该出自哪个地区呢？与此器同出的金银器共有200多件，从各器物上的铭文可知，这些器物是辽圣宗太平四年(公元1024年)至太平六年(公元1026年)间武定军节度使张俭上供给文忠王府的，武定军设在奉圣州，即今河北涿鹿，由此分析，这批器物可能出自涿鹿，流散到国外后，被戴狄安先生在英国重金收购。为辽皇室用物，制作于辽代强盛时期。

Cube-shaped casket with design of a rabbit

Liao dynasty (907～1125). Donated by French Connoisseur Christian Deydier in 1993. Silver with gilding. Height: 6.8 cm, side length of base: 7.4 cm, weight: 713 g.

133 **银棺、银宝函**

宋(公元960～1279年)。2001年2月陕西历史博物馆征集。银棺通高13.3厘米，长18.5厘米，宽9.5厘米，重471克（内放沙砾)。银宝函高6.5厘米，底边长5.5厘米，重79.5克。金棺银椁是佛教僧人安葬佛舍利(遗骨)的葬具。唐宋时期，供养舍利的风气极其盛行，讲究使用金银制作的容器，并将其制作成中国传统的棺椁形制。这件银棺采用捶揲、焊接、铆接、錾刻、编累等工艺制作，代表了宋代金银器制作的水平。

Coffin-shaped reliquary and cube-shaped casket

Song dynasty (960～1279). Collected by Shaanxi History Museum in 2001. Silver. Coffin: total height: 13.3 cm, length: 18.5 cm, width: 9.5 cm, weight: 471 g (with grit). Casket: height: 6.5 cm, side length of base: 5.5 cm, weight: 79.5 cm.

134 **金狗**

春秋(公元前770年～公元前476年)。1986年陕西省凤翔县秦公一号大墓出土。1991年4月从陕西省考古所雍城考古队调拨。高1.9厘米，长3.2厘米，重14克。金狗为实心，浇铸成型，身体及底部中线处有浅浅的范痕。从造型看，似为插在别的器物上的附件。

Dog

Spring and Autumn period (770～476 B.C.). Excavated from tomb 1 of Duck Qin, Fengxiang in 1986. Allocated from Yongcheng Archaeological Station of Shaanxi Archaeological Institute in 1991. Gold. Height: 1.9 cm, length: 3.2 cm, weight: 14 g.

135 **金啄木鸟**

春秋(公元前770年～公元前476年)。1986年陕西省凤翔县秦公一号大墓出土。1991年4月从陕西省考古所雍城考古队调拨。高1.6厘米，长1.1厘米，宽0.7厘米，重6克。浇铸成型，冠、身、翅、尾处均刻出细部装饰，在眼睛处原来似乎填有宝石。从造型来看，可能是冠上的装饰物。

Woodpecker

Spring and Autumn period (770～476 B.C.). Excavated from tomb 1 of Duck Qin, Fengxiang in 1986. Allocated from Yongcheng Archaeological Station of Shaanxi Archaeological Institute in 1991. Gold. Height: 1.6 cm, length: 1.1 cm, width: 0.7 cm, weight: 6 g.

136 **金羊虎饰**

春秋(公元前770年～公元前476年)。1986年陕西省凤翔县秦公一号大墓出土。1991年4月从陕西省考古所雍城考古队调拨。高2.6厘米，长3.5厘米，宽2.4厘米，重28克。浇铸成型，从背面留有的细柱状钉来看，似乎是插在别的器物上的附件。

Goat-and-tiger-shaped ornament

Spring and Autumn period (770～476 B.C.). Excavated from tomb 1 of Duck Qin, Fengxiang in 1986. Allocated from Yongcheng Archaeological Station of Shaanxi Archaeological Institute in 1991. Gold. Height: 2.6 cm, length: 3.5 cm, width: 2.4 cm, weight: 28 g.

137 **金兽形饰**

春秋(公元前770年～公元前476年)。1986年陕西省凤翔县秦雍城遗址出土。1991年6月从陕西省凤翔县博物馆调拨。高2.5厘米，长4.4厘米，宽3.8厘米，重58克。从内侧痕迹来看，为浇铸成型。正面兽面以鼻为中心，左右对称，兽首处有磨损痕迹。

Beast-shaped ornament

Spring and Autumn period (770～476 B.C.). Excavated from tomb 1 of Duck Qin, Fengxiang in 1986. Allocated from Fengxiang County Museum in 1991.Gold. Height: 2.5 cm, length: 4.4 cm, width: 3.8cm, weight: 58 g.

138 **双鹿纹金牌饰**

汉(公元前206年～公元220年)。1965年甘肃省通渭县堡子村村民捐。长10.1厘米，宽6.6厘米，重36克。纹饰由锥刺法戳出的圆点组成，显得十分拙朴。

Plaque with design of two deer

Han dynasty (206 B.C.～A.D. 220). Donated by a villager of Buzicun, Tongwei, Gansu in 1965. Gold. Length: 10.1 cm, width: 6.6 cm, weight: 36 g.

139 **双驼纹金牌饰**

汉(公元前206年～公元220年)。1974年陕西省西安市北郊龙首村出土。长6.9厘米，宽4.2厘米，重81克。

Plaque with design of two camels

Han dynasty (206 B.C.～A.D. 220). Excavated at Longshou village, northern suburbs of Xi'an city in 1974. Gold. Length: 6.9 cm, width: 4.2 cm, weight: 81 g.

140 **双鹿纹金牌饰**

汉(公元前206年～公元220年)。1987年甘肃省长庆油田水电厂交。长8.7厘米，宽6.3厘米，重63克。

Plaque with design of two deer

Han dynasty (206 B.C.～A.D. 220). Handed by the Water and Electricity Factory of Changqing Oilfield, Gansu in 1987. Gold. Length: 8.7 cm, width: 6.3 cm, weight: 63 g.

141 **银虎**

战国～汉(公元前475年～公元220年)。1957年陕西省神木县纳林高兔村出土。1991年3月从神木县文管会调拨。高7厘米，长12厘米，重88克。银虎为浇铸成型，壁厚0.1厘米，表面有模具留下的棱状痕迹。尾部有三个、颈部有一个规整的圆孔，似为穿线或铆钉所用，外壁有加工磨光痕迹。为匈奴人遗物。

Tiger

Warring States period～ Han dynasty (475 B.C.～A.D. 220). Excavated at Gaotu village, Nalin, Shenmu in 1957. Allocated from the Cultural Relics Committee of Shenmu in 1991. Silver. Length: 7 cm, width: 12 cm, weight: 88 g.

142 **银卧鹿**

战国～汉(公元前475年～公元220年)。1958年陕西省神木县纳林高兔村出土。1991年3月从神木县文管会调拨。高6.7厘米，长8.4厘米，重70克。浇铸成型，造型极其生动，是匈奴人的遗物。

Crouching deer

Warring States period～Han dynasty (475 B.C.～A.D. 220). Excavated at Gaotu village, Nalin, Shenmu in 1958. Allocated from the Cultural Relics Committee of Shenmu in 1991. Silver. height: 6.7 cm, Length: 8.4 cm, weight: 70 g.

143 A-B **金鹿形怪兽**

战国～汉(公元前475年～公元220年)。1958年陕西省神木县纳林高兔村出土。1991年3月从神木县文管会调拨。高12厘米，长11厘米，底座宽8厘米，重160克。金鹿形怪兽是用厚约0.12厘米的金片捶打制成的，鹿身中空，上有捶打出的突棱。底座为四瓣形，厚0.1厘米。每瓣上有三孔，原来可能是固定在别的器物上的。从造型看，是匈奴人遗物。

Dear-shaped monster

Warring States period～Han dynasty (475 B.C.～A.D. 220年). Excavated at Gaotu village, Nalin, Shenmu in 1957. Allocated from the Cultural Relics Committee of Shenmu in 1991. Gold. Height: 12 cm, Length: 11 cm, weight: 160 g.

144 **金马形饰件(2件)**

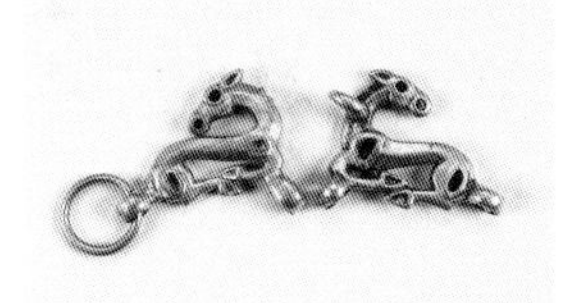

汉(公元前206年～公元220年)。1971年陕西省横山县出土。其一通长6.1厘米，重46克；其二通长5.1厘米，重38克。

Horse-shaped ornaments (2 pieces)

Han dynasty (206 B.C.～A.D. 220). Excavated in Hengshan in 1971. Gold. Length: 5.1～6.1cm, weight: 38～46g.

145 **金龙(4条)**

唐(公元618～907年)。1970年10月陕西省西安市南郊何家村基建工地唐代窖藏出土。其一高2.9厘米，长3.9厘米，重4克；其二高2.1厘米，长4.2厘米，重4克；其三高2.1厘米，长4.1厘米，重4克；其四高2.7厘米，长4.2厘米，重4克。金龙用金条折弯、切剪制成。头部触角是用0.05厘米细的金丝弯曲制成然后焊到头部凹槽内的。

Dragons (4 pieces)

Tang dynasty (618～907). Excavated at Hejiacun building site, southern suburbs of Xi'an city in 1970. Gold. Height: 2.1～2.9cm, length: 3.9～4.2cm, weight: 4g.

146 **鎏金铁芯铜龙**

唐(公元618～907年)。1975年陕西省西安市南郊草场坡出土。通高36.9厘米，最宽处10.5厘米，重2780克。中国古代，龙被视为祥瑞之物，也是王权的象征。此龙出土于唐长安城永乐坊东南隅，玄宗时期，此处是宰相燕国公张说的宅第。文献记载，法师

曾告诉张说，其宅西北处有王气，不宜取土。一个月后，法师又告诉张说，其地被取土，恐有祸事。埋龙于地，可能就是为了恢复王气，达到消灾免祸、祈福求瑞的目的。

Dragon with an iron core

Tang dynasty (618～907). Excavated at Caochangpo, southern suburbs of Xi'an city in 1975. Gilded copper with iron core. Total height: 36.9 cm, the widest part: 10.5 cm, weight: 2780 g.

147 **鎏金刻花铜羊**

唐(公元618～907年)。1974年陕西省西安市南郊红庙村出土。高9.4厘米，长15.8厘米，重1200克。浇铸成型，青铜表面鎏金。山羊伏于台座上，前腿一伸一屈，姿态安详。方座四面装饰海棠图案，空白处填疏松的鱼子地纹。内腔中空，方座内壁有几处尖棱状突起物，估计原来应有填充物。从其造型来看，当为铜镇。

Goat

Tang dynasty (618～907). Excavated at Hongmiao village, southern suburbs of Xi’an city in 1974. Height: 9.4 cm, length: 15.8 cm, weight: 1200 g.

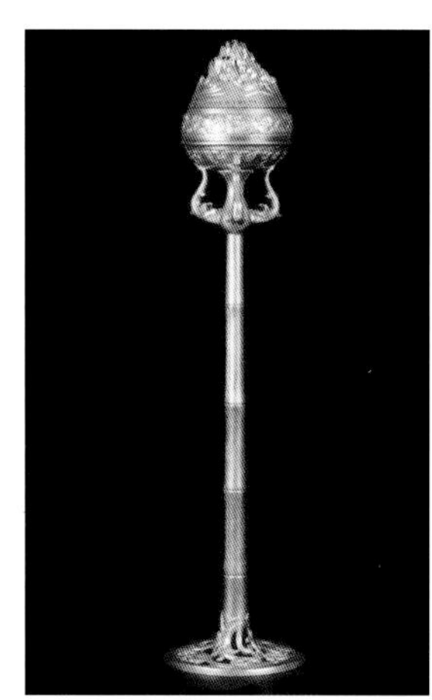

148 **鎏金银铜竹节熏炉**

西汉(公元前206年～公元9年)。1981年陕西省兴平县茂陵一号无名冢从葬坑出土。1991年3月从茂陵博物馆调拨。高58厘米，底径13.3厘米，口径9厘米，重2570克。炉盖口外侧刻铭文一周35字：“内者未央尚卧金黄涂竹节熏炉一具并重十斤十二两四年内官造五年十月输第初三”。底座圈足外侧刻铭文33字：“内者未央尚卧金黄涂竹节熏炉一具并重十一斤四年寺工造五年十月输第初四”。熏炉盖如博山，是汉代最为流行的博山炉造型，从熏炉上的铭文以及同出的其他器物上的铭文得知，这件熏炉原为汉未央宫之物，后赏赐给“阳信家”所有，因此推测，熏炉可能是汉武帝给他姐姐阳信长公主及其丈夫大将军卫青的赏品，是珍贵的汉代宫廷用物。

Bamboo-joint-shaped censer

Western Han dynasty (206 B.C.～A.D. 9). Excavated from anonymous satellite tomb 1, Maoling mausoleum, Xingping in 1981. Bronze, gilded and silvered. Height: 58 cm, diameter of mouth: 9 cm, diameter of foot: 13.3 cm, weight: 2570 g.

149 **鎏金铜虎形镇(2对)**

汉(公元前206年～公元220年)。1982年西安东郊三店村汉墓出土。高3.4厘米，长8.6厘米，宽6.8厘米，分别重843克、850克、857克、840克。四件两两相对，形制相同。伏虎前爪并屈于颌下，躬身侧伏，一只后足蜷于腹侧，露出尾巴，似在小憩，但猛兽直立的双耳，警觉的眼神，使人感到有随时腾身而起、捕捉猎物的力量。通体鎏金，实心较重。古代多用铜铁或玉石制成镇以压纸、压书或压席，造型“亦多肖生物者”。

Paper weights in tiger shape (2 pairs)

Han dynasty (206 B.C.～A.D. 220). Excavated from a Han tomb, eastern suburbs of Xi’an city in 1982. Height: 3.4 cm, Width: 6.8 cm, length: 8.6 cm, weight: 840～857 g.

150 **鎏金铜铺首(1对)**

汉(公元前206年～公元220年)。高8.6厘米，宽9.4厘米，重463克。1982年西安东郊三店村汉墓出土。汉代铺首均为这种神秘的兽首形，有冠有角，瞪目弯鼻，前足伸于嘴前，爪尖毕露，面目狞狰。背面正中有一长方形榫头，与鼻子的后部共同固定在门上，鼻子前端弯折处悬挂门环。

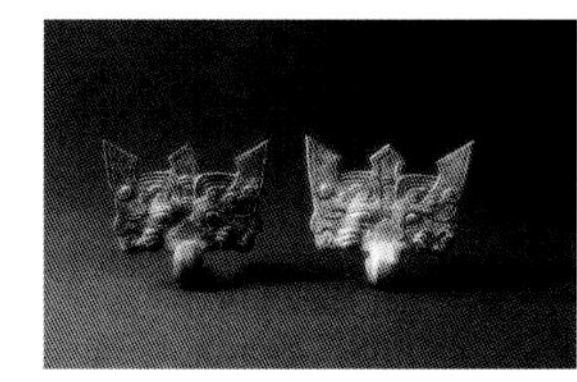

Door-knockers (a pair)

Han dynasty (206 B.C.～A.D. 220). Excavated from a Han tomb, Sandian village, eastern suburbs of Xi'an city in 1982. Height: 8.6 cm, width: 9.4 cm, weight: 463 g.

151 **鎏金铜铺首**

唐(公元618～907年)。1976年西安市大明宫遗址出土。直径26.2厘米，重413克。铜质鎏金，是宫殿大门上的铺首，嘴中铜环已失。造型极有气势，兽首如巨狮，獠牙巨口，睛暴髯张，作怒吼状，额上弯角如龙，当是神兽，置宫门之上，取辟邪之意。

Door-knocker

Tang dynasty (618～907). Excavated from the remains of Daming Palace, northern suburbs of Xi'an city in 1976. Diameter: 26.2 cm, weight: 413 g.

152 **桃形忍冬纹镂空五足银熏炉**

唐(公元618～907年)。1970年10月陕西省西安市南郊何家村基建工地唐代窖藏出土。通高30.5厘米，最大径21.5厘米，盖径16.6厘米，重4100克。炉身为三层套接而成，盖和肩部都透雕五组桃形忍冬花图案。下层炉盘心处墨书“三层五斤半”5字。熏炉也叫香炉，用它来焚烧香料，可以抑菌除秽、醒脑怡神、净化环境，是社会文明的一个重要内容。

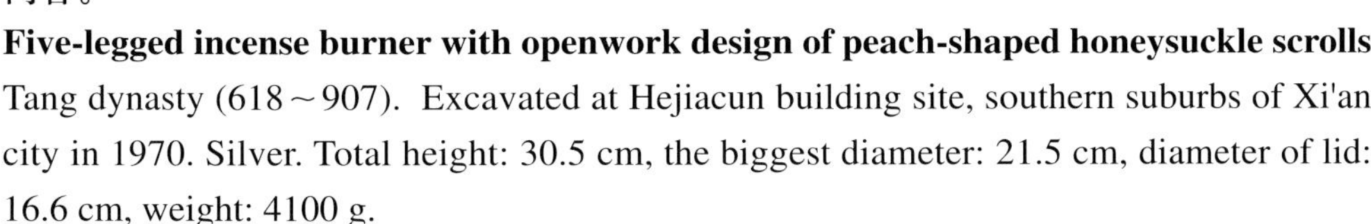

Five-legged incense burner with openwork design of peach-shaped honeysuckle scrolls

Tang dynasty (618～907). Excavated at Hejiacun building site, southern suburbs of Xi'an city in 1970. Silver. Total height: 30.5 cm, the biggest diameter: 21.5 cm, diameter of lid: 16.6 cm, weight: 4100 g.

153A-B **镂空飞鸟葡萄纹银香囊**

唐(公元618～907年)。1970年10月陕西省西安市南郊何家村基建工地唐代窖藏出土。直径4.7厘米，链长7.4厘米，焚香金盂径2.8厘米，重36克。香囊是用来香熏衣被、改善空气的卫生用具。外为镂空透雕花纹的球体，上下半球铰链相连，子母口扣合。球内是由两个同心圆的机环和一个纯金香盂构成的机械结构。无论是室内悬挂还是随身佩带，利用地心引力和活轴的平衡原理，使香囊转向任何角度，都不会倾覆而撒出香灰。唐代，贵族妇女还将佛经放在香囊中佩带于身，以求消灾避难，吉祥平安。

Perfumer with openwork design of flying birds and grapes

Tang dynasty (618～907). Excavated at Hejiacun building site, southern suburbs of Xi'an city in 1970. Silver. Diameter: 4.7 cm, length of chain: 7.4 cm, diameter of gold bowl: 2.8 cm, weight: 36 g.

154 **鎏金莲花形银灯头**

唐(公元618～907年)。1970年10月陕西省西安市南郊何家村基建工地唐代窖藏出土。高1.5厘米，口径3.5厘米，重73．5克。

Lotus-flower-shaped lamp top

Tang dynasty (618～907). Excavated at Hejiacun building site, southern suburbs of Xi'an city in 1970. Silver with gilding. Height: 1.5 cm, diameter of mouth: 3.5 cm, weight: 73.5 g.

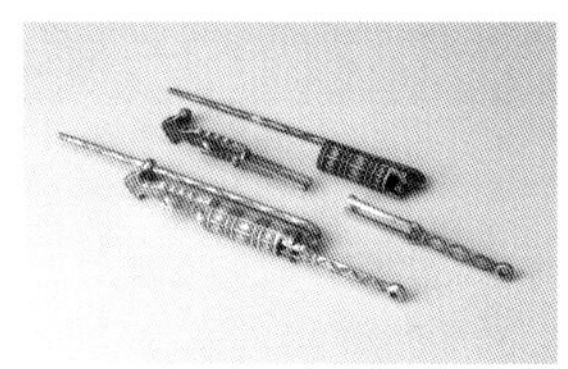

155 鎏金菱纹银锁(2件)

唐(公元618～907年)。1970年10月陕西省西安市南郊何家村基建工地唐代窖藏出土。其一通长18.4厘米，钥匙长7.8厘米，重85克；其二通长18.4厘米，钥匙长7.9厘米，重90克。分锁和钥匙两部分，出土时仍开锁自如，尚能使用，这种造型的锁一直延续到近现代。

Padlocks with design of rhombuses (2 pairs)

Tang dynasty (618～907). Excavated at Hejiacun building site, southern suburbs of Xi'an city in 1970. Silver with gilding. Total length: 18.4 cm, length of key: 7.8～7.9 cm, weight: 85～ 90 g.

156 鎏金鸿雁纹银渣斗

唐(公元618～907年)。1982年1月陕西省文物商店移交。通高15.7厘米，口径16.7厘米，底径8.5厘米，重391克。渣斗又叫唾盂、唾壶，是卫生用具。此渣斗从其制作看，似为晚唐时民间制作。

Spittoon with design of wild geese

Tang dynasty (618～907). Handed in by the Cultural Relics Store of Xi'an city in 1982. Silver with gilding. Total height: 15.7 cm, diameter of mouth: 16.7 cm, diameter of foot: 8.5 cm, weight: 391 g.

157 四鸾衔绶纹金银平脱铜镜

唐(公元618～907年)。1965年陕西省西安市东郊长乐坡出土。直径23厘米，厚0.55厘米，缘厚0.7厘米。铜镜是中国古代金属器物中沿用时间最长、使用范围最广、对人们日常生活影响最多的一种用具。唐代铜镜的制作和装饰空前繁荣，出现许多令人耳目一新的特种工艺镜。这种铜镜将金片、银片剪裁成花鸟形状，用黑漆粘贴在镜背上，空白处反复填漆，然后打磨，使黑色的漆底和黄白的纹样形成强烈的对比，产生飘逸、流动、华丽的装饰效果，是唐镜中一朵绚丽的奇葩。

Mirror with inlaid gold and silver design of four phoenixes holding ribbons in their mouths

Tang dynasty (618～907). Excavated at Changlepo, eastern suburbs of Xi'an city in 1965. Bronze. Diameter: 23 cm, thickness: 0.55 cm.

图书在版编目(CIP)数据

金银器／申秦雁编．—西安：陕西人民美术出版社，
2003.7
（陕西历史博物馆珍藏）
ISBN7-5368-1688-X

Ⅰ.金... Ⅱ.申... Ⅲ.金银器(考古)—中国—古代
Ⅳ.K876.43

中国版本图书馆 CIP 数据核字(2003)第 047829 号

责任编辑　李星明　胡耀辉
装帧设计　李星明

金银器

陕西历史博物馆珍藏
主编　申秦雁
陕西人民美术出版社出版发行
（西安北大街131号）
新华书店经销　深圳华新彩印制版有限责任公司印刷
889×1194毫米　16开本　12印张　100千字
2003年11月第1版　2003年11月第1次印刷
印数：1-3000

ISBN7-5368-1688-X/J·1333
定价：180.00元